From Pain to Parenthood

A Journey Through Miscarriage to Adoption

By Deanna Kahler

D1056961

DEDICATION

I dedicate this book to all those who have lost a baby to miscarriage. I understand your pain and heartbreak and want you to know that you are not alone. I sincerely hope this book will provide much-needed reassurance, encouragement, and hope in your journey to heal and one day become a parent.

"The human spirit is stronger than anything that can happen to it."
—C. C. Scott

CONTENTS

ACKNOWLEDGMENTS

With love and gratitude, I thank all those who have believed in me and offered their support and encouragement through the years. This list includes my family, friends, teachers, mentors, supervisors, and coworkers. There are far too many of you to mention, but you know who you are. Please know that you have all played a role in shaping me into the person and writer I am today. I have been blessed to have you in my life!

A special thanks to my husband Paul: your love, patience, understanding, and constructive criticism (otherwise known as brutal honesty) have helped me grow and evolve.

To my precious daughter, Katie: you are my light and my inspiration. Your vibrant personality, warm smile, enthusiasm, and compassion always remind me of what is most important in life.

To my parents, my sister, and the rest of my extended family: thank you for being there through both the rough times and the good times. I cherish my relationships with you all. I love you guys with all my heart!

Thank you also to all those who offered their assistance with this book, whether by proofreading, providing feedback, or sharing a personal story. To the adoptive parents who agreed to share their experiences and insights in this book, I am very appreciative. Your stories are touching and inspiring and will help others better understand miscarriage and adoption.

I also wish to acknowledge our awesome adoption agency staff and social worker for their support and guidance. Thank you for your patience and understanding. You helped our journey go as smoothly as possible. Without you, we would have never found our precious daughter.

And finally, to our daughter's birth parents: we will be forever grateful that you entrusted us to love and care for the most amazing child. Thank you for giving us this incredible experience!

"Strength does not come from winning;
your struggles develop your strength.
When you go through hardships and decide
not to surrender, that is strength."
—Mahatma Gandhi

PREFACE

Who we are and what we've been through in our lives is often not apparent to others. We do our best to navigate through life, make the right decisions, and cope with adversity. Sometimes we look around at our friends and think, "That person is really lucky and has a great life!" While this may be true, we often fail to remember that everyone has their own set of struggles, challenges, and disappointments. Many people prefer to keep these problems to themselves, for fear of burdening others or not living up to someone else's standards or expectations. But as I've learned in my own life, often these issues turn out to be not only an opportunity for growth, but also a way to help others who are facing the same challenges.

First, let me say that I am indeed lucky, and I do have a great life! I have a loving, supportive husband and a sweet, smart, and beautiful daughter. I live in a nice house in a good neighborhood. I had a successful career as a writer and editor before my daughter was born. I feel grateful every day for all of the wonderful blessings in my life. But that isn't my whole story. Like everyone else in this world, I've had my share of heartbreaks and disappointments. Some would be amazed at all I have been through!

What I've encountered, however, is not as important as what I'm going to do with these experiences. I feel that my struggles and the way I've handled them are important lessons for others. I believe I have something to offer the world by sharing my story.

Throughout this book, you will see what I believe are the most important attributes when faced with a major life challenge—strength, perseverance, and faith. I must admit I didn't always feel like I was strong or determined, especially during my lowest points. There were times when I lacked faith and doubted whether or not everything would work out. I eventually learned that this is okay. We can't always be strong. Sometimes we need to fall apart before we can put ourselves back together. You gain strength by fully experiencing your emotions and then working through them.

Anyone who's struggled with miscarriages or infertility knows it's a tough road filled with pain and emptiness. Losing a baby tears your world apart and turns your life upside down. You will be sad. You will be angry. You will grieve your loss. Unfortunately, those who haven't been through it often don't understand.

The good news is that there are many women out there who *do* understand and have been through the trauma of losing a baby. I am one of them. I'm a mother to an amazing child, but the road to parenthood was paved with obstacles, some that seemed insurmountable at times. I've endured the pain of my loss, and I've faced many struggles to have what I want in life. I know there are plenty of others out there who are in pain, who desperately long for a child to love and often feel like that day will never come. I've been there. I understand. And I'm here to share my story in the hopes that those who are going through the same struggles will know they are not alone and that it is possible to have the child they so desire.

Of course, telling such a personal story is never easy. I must admit when I first sat down to write this book, I was a bit apprehensive to unleash the emotions, turmoil, and fear that I went through following my miscarriages. My first miscarriage especially was a very difficult time in my life and one that I didn't talk openly about with anyone except close family members and friends. I kept a lot inside and carried the pain and grief of my loss around with me for a very long time. I learned firsthand just how profoundly losing a baby can affect both your mind and body. I honestly can say that I was a complete emotional wreck for a while. Did I really want to share something so personal with the world? What would others think of me? Would they view me as weak?

But the more I thought about it, the more I realized that what matters most to me is helping people. I want to make a difference in the lives of others. I want to share my story as a way of reaching out to women in need. Miscarriage is a difficult road filled with much heartbreak. And no one should have to go through it alone.

I also realized that what I'm about to share doesn't show my weakness—it shows my strength. It takes great strength to overcome what I did. And, it takes even greater strength to write what is in your heart for all to see. I truly believe that by doing so, I can touch the lives of others. I hope to be a source of inspiration and encouragement, as I share the dark place I came from and how I eventually ended up in a place of abundant joy, unconditional love, and parental bliss. I want to show those who are having difficulty having a baby that adoption is a wonderful alternative. Finally, I hope to open people's eyes to the struggles and suffering some endure after a miscarriage and help educate others on the often misunderstood adoption process.

My heart goes out to all who have experienced the loss of a baby. This book is dedicated to you.

I'm here to show you that no matter what happens, there is always hope. The pain will lessen. The tears will dry. You will feel whole again—no matter how you are feeling now. I'm living proof of that. Come join me for a real-life story of loss, grief, struggles, triumph, and unconditional love. I invite you to follow my journey...from pain to parenthood.

My Child

I've wished for you for many years
Searched near and far, cried many tears
Devoted my life to finding you
You're out there somewhere—I know it's true

I cannot see you, but I can feel
My love for you is very real
The wait's been long and sometimes rough
Some days I think I've had enough

But somehow I still hang on tight
I know in my heart that this is right
Yet unknown and still unseen
You'll come home one day, fulfill my dream

(—Deanna Kahler, 10/24/05)

*"Each new life, no matter how fragile or brief,
forever changes the world."*
—*Author Unknown*

CHAPTER 1: AN INCONCEIVABLE LOSS

When you find out you're pregnant for the first time, there are no words to describe how you feel. It's a big moment filled with both excitement and a little fear. From choosing baby names to picking out cute little clothes, your life becomes a whirlwind of eager anticipation.

When I found out I was pregnant in 1999, I was so excited! I had always dreamed of the day I would become a mom and had hoped to have a daughter someday. I envisioned all of the cool things my husband and I would do with our child. I imagined holding and rocking my daughter to sleep at night, pushing her on the swing, feeding the ducks at the park, reading bedtime stories, visiting the zoo, and helping her learn and grow. Being pregnant made these thoughts so much more real. It was finally going to happen!

Like many newly pregnant women, I was eager to share the happy news with friends and family. Since I found out I was pregnant after just a couple of weeks, it was very early in the pregnancy. But that didn't matter. I was so thrilled that I just couldn't keep my excitement to myself. Besides, when you're a healthy, young woman, you never expect that anything could go wrong.

I visited my doctor, who confirmed the pregnancy and estimated a due date of December 2. This would be just in time for Christmas! Oh, what an incredible feeling to imagine your first holiday with your child! It would no doubt be the best Christmas anyone could ask for. It all seemed like a dream come true. Everything was perfect.

Confident that all was well, I immediately started preparing for motherhood. I read *What to Expect When You're Expecting*. I also bought my husband the book *She's Having a Baby and I'm Having a Nervous Breakdown*. Even though we had agreed to give up birth control, I don't think he had expected that I would become pregnant so quickly. The poor guy seemed in a state of shock and was actually terrified by the idea of becoming a father and being responsible for a tiny, helpless infant. I tried to reassure him that we would be good parents and helped him focus on the fun and positive aspects of parenthood.

One activity we particularly enjoyed was flipping through the baby name book and discussing our preferences. Some of my favorites were Kristen Lea, Kara Rose, and Connor John. I also loved Alyssa and Calista. Paul was more interested in the traditional names, such as Christine and Katherine. Although we did not agree on most name choices, we eventually narrowed down our list.

In addition to having fun discussing names, Paul and I also browsed through catalogs, getting ideas for furniture and bedding. I saw a beautiful and unique round crib that had a canopy. It was just adorable! The crib reminded me of a little castle fit for a prince or princess.

I looked forward to the day when I could finally decorate the nursery. "It won't be long now," I thought. Motherhood was more than just a dream now; it was real. I couldn't wait for the fabulous life I was soon going to live. For several weeks, I thought about my growing baby. I imagined what it would be like to hold her and kiss her soft cheek. I tried to picture what she might look like. I imagined feeding her, dressing her in cute little outfits, reading her bedtime stories, and teaching her how to talk and walk. I thought about the family trips we would take and visits to the park and beach. I envisioned sharing the beauty of the world with her. During this time, I also began developing a bond with my baby and could already feel the motherly instincts and love coming on full force. I basically had mapped out the first couple years of my unborn child's life. Then everything changed.

Maybe my excitement and preparation was a little premature. Maybe it would have been better to guard my heart until I was certain. But when it's your first pregnancy, you don't think or expect that it won't actually happen. After all, no one in my family had ever miscarried, so there was no reason to believe I was at risk. But unfortunately I was.

The first indication was when Paul and I went to dinner at Chili's restaurant one night. I started having sharp abdominal pains in the parking lot. The pain was unlike anything I had experienced, so I became worried there was a problem with the pregnancy. I called my family doctor right away, who suggested I head to the emergency room to be safe. After spending a few hours in the ER and having various tests, the doctors could not find anything wrong and sent me home. I was so relieved and decided the pain must have been caused by something simple, like my muscles stretching or gas. I went to bed that night happy and relieved that all was well.

Unfortunately, that was not the last sign that something was amiss. Just a couple of weeks later, while at work, I went into the bathroom stall and was horrified to discover I was bleeding! A wave of fear came over me that sent an electric shock through my body, and I knew at that moment that my dreams of becoming a mother were about to be shattered. I was so upset and shaken that I couldn't even drive myself home from work. Thankfully, two coworkers, Kim and CeAnne, came to my aid. One drove my car and me, and the other followed in her car. I really don't remember the ride home. It's all just a blur now. However, I do remember as we pulled into the driveway, my friends told me if I needed anything to just ask. They were very sincere and concerned for me, and I was touched by their kindness. I thanked them and appreciated the offer, although I knew I would not be calling on them. I always had a hard time asking for help and never liked to bother or burden others with my troubles. After they left, I found myself sitting on the couch in the family room, alone, scared, and uncertain of what lay ahead.

I made an appointment with my OB/GYN to confirm what I already knew deep in my heart. The doctor examined me and explained that during a miscarriage, the cervix dilates just like it does when you're about to give birth. She pointed out that my cervix was not dilated, which was a good sign. However, since I was bleeding, there was still cause for alarm. The only way to find out for sure what was going on was to have an ultrasound. The doctor sent me over to the hospital and put a rush on the results. She promised to call as soon as she heard anything.

Later that night, as my husband and I were driving home from dinner, my doctor called my cell phone. She said she was sorry, but the ultrasound confirmed that I was miscarrying. She told me to let her know if I needed anything. She explained that often the body takes care of things itself, but if I experienced any severe bleeding to call her right away. As I listened to the doctor's words, I felt disconnected and numb. At that moment, I felt like I was watching someone else's life. When you find out you will never be able to hold or meet the baby you're carrying, you feel like your world has come to a screeching halt. It's like someone has pushed the pause button on your life. The whole thing just didn't seem real. How could this be happening?

In the days that followed, the bleeding continued. Every time I would see the blood, I couldn't help but think I was losing my child slowly bit by bit. It wasn't just ordinary bleeding; it was the end of my baby's life. It was the end of my dream to become a mom. I was devastated. I felt so lost and alone. Unfortunately, my husband didn't seem to understand or be able to comfort me. To him, the baby was not even real yet. And since he was actually afraid of becoming a dad, I think in some ways he was relieved that it didn't work out. In my mind, I had lost a child. Someone important to me had died, and I was grieving. The hard part is that I was grieving alone with no one to share my sorrow.

This is often a problem for women who miscarry. You feel so sad and devastated, but many times your friends and family don't get it. They don't realize how much love you can feel for a baby you never saw, met, or held. You try to turn to those you love for comfort and support, but they have little to offer you during the time when you need someone to lean on the most. It's not that they don't want to help or that they don't care. No one wants to see you sad or hurting. They just don't understand what you are feeling and the intensity of your emotions.

Even the words they say to you can come across as insensitive or hurtful. They often dismiss your grief and trivialize your pain, all the while thinking they are being encouraging and supportive. A couple of people, who thought they were being helpful, acted as if the whole thing was no big deal. I remember them saying, "Oh well. I guess it wasn't meant to be." "Maybe there was something wrong with the baby." "You can always try again."

Those who have lost a baby to miscarriage know that those words hurt. No woman wants to hear that she was "meant" to lose a child or that she can always try again. When you lose a baby, the last thing you want to think about is trying again. I certainly didn't want to ever feel the pain I was feeling at that moment. And I didn't want another baby. I wanted *that* one. I wanted the one I thought I was having...the one I was carrying inside of me and had such big plans and dreams for.

As you know, life doesn't always work out the way you plan. Sometimes there are unexpected heartbreaks and struggles. Sometimes your body fails you and doesn't do what it is supposed to do. In my case, not only did my body not support my developing child, but it also didn't know how to let go and heal naturally.

After a few days, the bleeding became much heavier. One night I had a dream I was in surgery and was losing consciousness. In my dream I thought I was dying. I woke up afraid. Later that day, I began bleeding very heavily. I lay on the couch and tried to rest, but it didn't help. I knew right away there was a problem. I called to make an appointment with my OB/GYN. Unfortunately, she was out of the office. So I had to see a doctor I had only met once. My whole world just seemed out of my control. I felt sad, scared, and helpless. My sister and mom took me to the doctor's office because I was in need of moral support. On the way there, I told them I felt an emergency D&C (dilation and curettage) coming on. A D&C is a procedure where the cervix is widened and the contents of the uterus are surgically removed by scraping and/or scooping. It is sometimes used during miscarriage when they body is having difficulty shedding the tissue itself.

Once at the doctor's office, I nervously got settled into the exam room. The doctor was very quiet as he examined me. The sounds of large amounts of blood splattering against the table echoed through the room. It was disturbing and reminded me of something out of a horror film. How could I be bleeding that much?

Afterward, the doctor had a very serious look on his face and said to meet him across the street at the hospital. He said I was losing far too much blood and that he needed to perform an emergency D&C right away. Even though I expected this, I just stared in shock at him. I was afraid of having the procedure because I had never had any type of surgery before. He then asked if I had any questions. The only thing that came out of my mouth was "I don't want to die."

"That's why we need to do the surgery," he replied calmly.

Those words did not take away the shock and fear I was feeling. But I had no choice. Like it or not, I needed to have this procedure. I headed across the street to the hospital with my mom and sister right away. The nurses took me in fast and started prepping me for surgery. The anesthesiologist came in and explained that he would give me some medicine that would make me sleep and I would wake up when the D&C was over. I had never been under general anesthesia before and was afraid of something going wrong and never waking up. Remembering my dream the night before where I was losing consciousness and possibly dying, I protested.

"What if I don't want that?" I asked.

The doctor seemed surprised. He probably wasn't used to patients asking not to be put out for surgery. Most people don't want to be awake during a procedure. But I was different. I felt a need to protect myself. I wanted to be alert and aware of my surroundings and what was happening to me.

"Well, then, we can do a spinal," he said.

He explained he would insert a needle into my spine with medication that would numb me from the waist down. I would be awake during the whole procedure. The medication would last for several hours, and I would remain at the hospital until I was able to wiggle my toes and stand. I agreed to the spinal. At least I would be alert and conscious. Next, another doctor came in with some pills and a cup of liquid medication for me to swallow. Again, I questioned him.

"What are these for and why do I need them?" I asked.

He explained they were for my stomach and that some people throw up during the procedure. The medication was to help prevent this. After a few minutes, I reluctantly took the medicine. I often wondered if they thought I was a difficult patient. But when you're losing a baby and you feel like your life is spinning out of control, you do whatever you can to remain in charge of your life. I couldn't save my baby or control what my body was doing. But I could certainly make sure the medical treatment I received was on my terms.

Shortly after taking the medicine, a nurse came to take me down for the procedure. I remembered my dream the night before. Right before she wheeled me back, I whispered in my mom's ear.

"I had a dream about this last night. And, I don't think I made it..."

Then I was whisked off to the operating room. I can't imagine what my mother must have been thinking as I left her with that troubling thought. I wasn't trying to worry anyone, but I felt compelled to tell her about my dream in case I really did die. After all, I did dream about the surgery and that came to be. How did I know the part where I thought I was dying wouldn't come true too? It was clearly a very unpredictable time in my life, and I had no idea where it was all heading or what would happen next.

During the D&C, I remember hearing a lot of

noises as the doctors worked on me. They had a cloth curtain just above my waist, so I couldn't see anything that was going on. I was glad about that because I certainly didn't want to. The sight of blood has always been very disturbing to me. In fact, hospitals have also always bothered me. I have seen far too many people suffer and die in hospitals, so I never wanted to be in one because they always reminded me of illness and death.

What I had forgotten is that hospitals are also the place where a new life enters this world and where healing and recovery begin. So many doctors and nurses are ready to help people in any way they can. I experienced the positive, healing side of hospitals firsthand that day. I had the pleasure of meeting a couple of very kind and comforting nurses while I was undergoing my procedure. They helped ease my fears and talked to me the entire time. One held my hand and kept asking if I was okay. She agreed with my decision to have a spinal. She said that it was the best way and that she didn't blame me for not wanting to be under general anesthesia. She admitted that she wouldn't want to either. It was reassuring to hear that I wasn't the only one leery of being unconscious—even medical professionals don't like the idea!

Next, the nurse said that they were giving me a medication called Versed to help relax me and that it had an amnesia effect, so I may not remember anything about the surgery. Had she known me, she would have realized that I'm one of those rare people who would remember every detail. There was never a time during the procedure where I wasn't awake. Although I was given a pretty strong sedative, I was alert the entire time. It felt like an eternity until it was over!

After the D&C, I was wheeled to a general recovery room with other patients who had just undergone surgery. The nurse told me not to try sitting up because the spinal would likely give me a bad headache. As I lay there, I noticed that my body was trembling uncontrollably. I tried to stop, but I couldn't. I didn't know if the shaking was from fear, because I was cold, or for some other reason.

The nurse brought me a warm, white cotton blanket and covered me with it. It felt soothing and gave me some comfort. She also told me that shaking is a common side effect of the medication they had given me. It should wear off in a while. I asked if I could see my family, but she said she needed to monitor my vitals for a bit first. I continued to lie there while they monitored my heart rate, blood pressure, and oxygen saturation levels. During my time in recovery, I kept hearing the moaning sounds of a poor woman who had just had surgery. She sounded like she was in sheer agony, and my heart went out to her. Although I couldn't see her, I could feel her pain. A nurse kept saying to her over and over again, "Camille, it's okay. The surgery's over. You're in recovery."

I have no idea what type of surgery Camille had, but I hoped that she would recover well. No one should have to suffer like that. Hearing her cries reminded me once again of how fragile life is. At least she was in good hands.

Finally, after what seemed like forever, the nurse said I could see my family. Then she chuckled and added, "You must be excited because your blood pressure just went up!" Indeed, I was! She had no idea how eager I was to see my family. My mom and sister came in the room. Fortunately, they had reached my husband at work and told him what was going on, so he was there too! I was so relieved. I just wanted to go home to my nice warm bed and put the whole nightmare behind me.

Little did I know, doing that would be far more challenging that I had ever imagined. The experience of losing a child and having an emergency D&C would later resurface in a big way. The baby was gone. The surgery was over. But I was far from being done with the whole nightmare. This was just the beginning of my downward spiral.

"Faith includes noticing the mess,
the emptiness and discomfort,
and letting it be there until some light returns."
—Anne Lamont

CHAPTER 2: AT THE HEART OF IT ALL

After the miscarriage and surgery, my suffering unfortunately did not end. Now it was time to figure out what went wrong. When you miscarry, you want answers. Why did this happen to me? Is there anything I could have done to prevent it? Is it my fault? Could this happen again?

First and foremost, losing a baby is never your fault. You may feel responsible in some way because your body didn't do what it was supposed to. I remember thinking maybe I should have drank more water. Or maybe that medium-rare roast beef sandwich I ate at work was the cause. Perhaps I should have exercised. None of this had any bearing on the outcome of my pregnancy. You too may wonder if you had taken better care of yourself, if it would have made a difference. The answer is no. There is nothing you did to cause this, and nothing you could have done to prevent it. Miscarriages happen for a variety of reasons, most of which are medical in nature. They are also very common. According to the American Pregnancy Association's website, the chances of having a miscarriage range from 10 to 25 percent. These losses typically occur during the first trimester, and many times happen to healthy women. So please do yourself a favor and don't blame yourself for what happened. Placing blame will only make you feel worse and won't accomplish anything.

That doesn't mean you need to feel powerless over the situation. What you can do is have your doctor run some tests to see if there are any issues that could have contributed to the miscarriage. Often the cause is a random genetic problem in the developing baby. This can be determined by performing a chromosome analysis on the fetus to see if there are any abnormalities. Approximately 70 percent of early repeated miscarriages are caused by genetic abnormalities in the fetus. Another cause is a physical problem with the woman's uterus. Ten to 15 percent of women with recurrent miscarriages have uterine malformations. These can often be diagnosed using special tests such as a hysteroscopy, sonohysterogram, or hysterosalpingogram (HSG).

A hysteroscope allows your doctor to see

fibroids, polyps, or congenital uterine abnormalities by inserting a small, telescope-like device into the uterus and then filing the uterus with carbon dioxide or sterile saline. During a sonohysterogram, which is also called a hysterosonogram or 3-D saline sonogram, the uterus is filled and expanded with saline using a catheter and then a 3-D vaginal ultrasound is performed. Again, your doctor will be able to see abnormalities such as fibroids and polyps. Similarly, the HSG test provides your doctor with information about the internal structure of the fallopian tubes and uterus. During this outpatient procedure, dye is passed through a small tube through the cervix and into the uterus and sequential X-rays are performed. With this test, your doctor will be able to diagnose a tubal obstruction, fibroids, polyps, and congenital abnormalities of the uterus. All of these can interfere with a pregnancy and lead to miscarriage.

Other potential causes of pregnancy loss are thyroid problems, low progesterone levels, and various clotting disorders, all of which can be diagnosed by simple blood tests.

In my case, the doctor ordered blood work to determine the potential cause of my loss. I tested positive for anticardiolipin antibodies, an autoimmune problem, which can cause blood clots, miscarriages, heart attacks, and strokes. Normally, your body produces antibodies to fight off infections and diseases. In the case of autoantibodies, these disease fighters are directed at normal, healthy cells. Anticardiolipin antibodies interfere with blood vessel function, causing narrowing and irregularity of the vessels. Often, these antibodies cause recurrent miscarriages.

Definitely not something you want to hear. It was hard to accept that my own body was producing antibodies that interfered with my baby's development. I felt like my body had failed me in some way. This was certainly something that needed to be addressed. When you find a problem that may have contributed to your miscarriage, it's important to see the appropriate specialists to assess the situation and determine a course of action for future pregnancies.

My doctor sent me to Henry Ford Hospital in downtown Detroit to see a perinatologist—a specialist in high-risk pregnancies. My husband went with me for moral support. The perinatologist said that my antibody levels were not really high, so that was good news. Someone with higher levels is at a greater risk of developing more serious problems, including issues with blood clots, heart attacks, and strokes. He also thought it was encouraging that I had never had a blood clot before. He said I would most likely need to be on baby aspirin before attempting another pregnancy and possibly even Heparin (an injectable blood thinner) during pregnancy. Since my issue was autoimmune in nature, a visit to a rheumatologist, a doctor who specializes in autoimmune disorders, would provide more information on my condition and the appropriate treatment.

Shortly after meeting with the perinatologist, I

visited a rheumatologist. After more tests, he verified that I did indeed have these abnormal antibodies. He also ran a more specific test called "Anti-Beta 2 Glycoprotein 1." These antibodies are strongly associated with thrombosis and pose a problem with pregnancy. I tested positive for them as well, so the doctor confirmed that I would most likely need to be treated with both Heparin and baby aspirin if I was to become pregnant again. In addition, I would need to be closely monitored by a perinatologist throughout the pregnancy and would be at risk for preeclampsia, preterm labor, a low birth weight baby, and bleeding problems during pregnancy and/or delivery. He also explained that my condition could cause blood clots and lead to heart attacks and strokes.

"I don't want to feel like a ticking time bomb," I said. "What can I do to decrease my risks?"

"You could take a baby aspirin a day now as a precaution," he replied.

I decided to start taking the aspirin to protect myself from potential health problems. I certainly didn't want any blood clots, heart attacks, or strokes. I was only thirty years old at the time and far too young to worry about such serious health issues. After hearing the disappointing news from the rheumatologist, I became very depressed. Not only did I lose a baby, I now knew for sure I had a problem that would likely cause miscarriage again if not treated. And to further add to my fears, this condition could also put my own health in jeopardy. This news was very hard to digest. I was still dealing with a pregnancy loss, and now I had to come to terms with a health concern as well. How could this be happening? Why me? None of this made any sense to me. It was all so overwhelming.

My grief affected my mind and body in ways I had never expected. Many of you who have lost a baby may have noticed this also. You may have felt unprepared for the intense emotions that a pregnancy loss leaves you with. You may have heard of others who have miscarried and felt sad for them, but until it happens to you, you have no idea the depth of the pain.

According to *The Women's Encyclopedia of Health and Emotional Healing,* "the length of the pregnancy is not as significant as how emotionally linked a woman feels to her baby." The book goes on to say that if you felt your child was real very early in the pregnancy, then you may experience as much grief as someone who has lost a newborn. If the love for your unborn child was already there, you will be heartbroken and devastated. Your loss can affect you in many different ways, some emotional and some physical. You may notice muscle tension, have trouble sleeping, have difficulty concentrating, suffer from frequent headaches, cry a lot, or even notice unusual sensations in your body.

Many women experience symptoms of depression following a pregnancy loss. Christina Molby, a stay-at-home mom from Michigan, endured an astounding eight miscarriages, four of which happened before giving birth to her daughter, and the others before adopting her son. She described the aftermath of her miscarriages as being in a fog. Christina suffered from depression and had difficulty sleeping. She said she never even realized just how depressed she was until she starting coming out of it.

Although unpleasant, these are normal responses to grief. You may also notice you feel anxious or afraid. And, because your body has let you down, you may become overly concerned about your own health. All of these things happened to me.

It began with an alarming symptom I noticed one night after seeing a movie with friends. My husband and I were talking in the movie theater parking lot with our friends Bill and Carrie after seeing the film *The Mummy*. Suddenly, I felt a huge flutter in my chest that lasted several seconds. It terrified me, and I feared there was something wrong with my heart. Now, it all makes sense to me. There was nothing wrong with my heart physically. I was suffering from a "broken heart" over the loss of my child. I was grieving. At the time, I didn't connect the two. I started having more and more of these sensations in my chest in the days that followed. I was afraid I was going to have a heart attack and die. After what the rheumatologist had told me about anticardiolipin antibodies and their potential effects on the body, my fear of a heart attack didn't seem very far-fetched. Understandably concerned, I went to my family doctor, who listened to my heart and performed an electrocardiogram (EKG), which measures the electrical activity of your heart and checks for potential problems. Everything was normal. The doctor told me the heart palpitations were from anxiety. And the cause of the anxiety was obviously the miscarriage and my fear of health problems.

Despite getting a clean bill of health, I continued to have many heart palpitations over the next two weeks. I still felt very sad and afraid, which left me physically, mentally, and emotionally drained. Then I caught a stomach flu. I was very sick and not eating or drinking much. My husband took me to the doctor on a Saturday morning. The doctor examined me and asked if I was still having the heart palpitations. I told her I was, and she decided to do another EKG. As I sat in the exam room with my husband waiting for the test results, I overheard the doctor talking about calling an ambulance and sending someone to the hospital. I started to cry and told my husband they were talking about me. I was sick, exhausted, and afraid. I didn't want to go to the hospital. I just wanted to go home. My husband didn't believe they were talking about me. He was sure they must have been referring to another patient and thought I was just freaking out for no reason.

As it turns out, I was right. The doctor came in and told me my EKG was abnormal and that they were calling an ambulance to take me to the hospital to monitor me for a heart attack. I asked if my husband could just take me, but she refused.

She said she wouldn't want anything to happen to me on the way there. She apologized and said she had no choice and that there were changes in my EKG from last time. So, much to my dismay, I was put on a stretcher and loaded into the back of an ambulance. I was once again alone and terrified of dying. As if losing a child wasn't bad enough, now I had to fear for my own life.

At the hospital, I wasn't allowed to get up—not even to go to the bathroom. I kept hearing alarms going off right next to me, which frightened me even more. To this day, I do not know what the alarms were for, although I suspect my heart rate was too fast. Every time an alarm went off, I feared I was having a heart attack. No one was telling me anything. So I asked a nurse who came to check on me, "Am I going to die?" She looked at me sympathetically and gently stroked my hair.

"No, sweetie," she said kindly. "You're not going to die. Your work here isn't finished yet."

Her words provided some comfort to me, and I will never forget that nurse. It was like an angel was sent to help me. She was one of the few people who seemed genuinely concerned about more than just my physical well-being. She actually cared how I felt and what I was going through. My husband and dad were both there also and offered their support and reassurance. But I also longed for my mom. She and I had always shared a close relationship. She is not only my mom, but also my friend. I felt safer, stronger, and more secure when she was around. Who better to understand a daughter's pain?

Unfortunately, my mother was on a plane to Las Vegas and could not be there for me. I felt so lost without her. My emotions were all over the place—and the residual pregnancy hormones running through my body didn't help! I felt angry, sad, frustrated, hopeless, and afraid. I just didn't know what to do with all that I was feeling.

It didn't help that the doctors and nurses weren't really telling me anything. I later learned that my family doctor believed the most likely cause of my abnormal EKG was dehydration from the flu, but they had to monitor me as a precaution to be absolutely certain it wasn't a problem with my heart. It would have been nice if someone had told *me* that! I spent hours thinking I might be having a heart attack because that is what they told me. I was scared, still grieving the loss of my baby, and desperately needing my mother's comfort. I was going through one of the most difficult times in my life. I needed all the support I could get. But apparently no one knew at that point just how deeply I was hurting and how afraid and alone I felt.

After several hours, the doctors at the hospital confirmed what my doctor had suspected. I was not having a heart attack. My heart was perfectly fine. My abnormal EKG was caused by dehydration. They gave me liquids by IV and later released me.

After my hospital scare, my anxiety became worse. Even though I turned out to be fine, the whole experience—combined with the miscarriage, emergency surgery, and abnormal clotting tests— was just too much for me. I became overly concerned about my health and every little symptom I noticed became cause for alarm. I suffered from huge panic attacks, sometimes lasting for hours. I had frequent heart palpitations, nausea, shaking, and trouble sleeping. Sometimes I would sit awake at night and just tremble for hours. Or I would pace the floors at three a.m., terrified that something bad was about to happen to me. Sometimes I suffered alone in silence in the middle of the night, afraid of disturbing my husband by waking him or upsetting my parents by calling them. Other times, my emotional pain was just so unbearable that I was desperate for some relief. I just wanted somebody—anybody—to help me. I wanted to run, to scream, to escape the nightmare that had become my life. At those moments of weakness, I would wake up my husband or call my mom hoping that maybe they could save me from my overwhelming fear and anxiety. Unfortunately, even though they tried to offer words of comfort and reassurance, no one knew how to reach me or how to relieve my pain.

I found it difficult to eat and lost a lot of weight. I would wake up every morning immediately overcome by extreme nausea. I always tried to fight it at first, but ended up dashing into the bathroom to throw up. I was afraid to be alone. I felt so frightened and on edge all the time. I thought there was something really wrong with me, and I was going to die. At one point, I was so consumed with grief and fear that I didn't even know if I had the will to live anymore. I felt like I had fallen down into a deep, dark pit and no one could reach me or help me get out. I was trapped in a terrifying world of my own, surrounded by overwhelming emotional pain. It was unbearable!

My husband tried to help, but didn't know what to do. He tried to convince me that I was okay, but I didn't believe him. I felt so awful, how could I possibly be all right? He became very frustrated and starting yelling at me and getting upset whenever I would have a panic attack. Along with dealing with the loss of my child and fears of having a heart attack, I became afraid I was going to lose my husband too. I feared he would get tired of dealing with me and leave. This just added to my anxiety and made me feel even worse.

I felt so alone and isolated—like no one could help me. I even started feeling like no one would miss me if I wasn't here. Everyone was frustrated with me, and I often felt like a burden or an inconvenience. It hurt to feel like I was always upsetting everyone. I wondered if maybe my family would be better off without me. I knew that I certainly couldn't stay on my current path. It was all just too much to bear. I was so exhausted from all of the fighting and struggling that I just wanted to give up. One day I even asked my husband if he would miss me if I wasn't around. He just looked at me in surprise and said, "Yes, of course, I would."

At the time, I honestly didn't know what his answer would be. All I knew is that I was trying to figure out if I should continue to try and get my life together or not. I wanted to know if my life was worth fighting for. I would never take my own life, but I would stop trying so hard to exist. I wasn't eating much at the time and was forcing myself to eat what little I could to survive. Living was a big effort for me back then. Some days I felt like it was easier to just give up.

Then one night something changed. At one of the lowest points in my life, I had a bizarre dream. In my dream, I floated out of my body where I lay in bed sleeping and drifted into our bathroom. I looked at myself in the mirror and was amazed to see that I was glowing white and surrounded by light. I looked so beautiful and peaceful. There was this energy all around me, and I thought to myself, "Deanna, you look angelic."

Next thing I knew, I was in a room that looked similar to a courtroom. It was filled with old men and women wearing long, flowing, light gray robes. They were all watching me intently and looked very concerned. As I gazed around the room, I spotted my grandpa, whom I had always called Papa. He had passed away the year before. Papa looked really worried and shook his head "no." He also gestured with his hand, waving me back. I knew at that moment, I wasn't supposed to be in that place. I had to go back and fight some more. I was supposed to live and go on. When I woke up, I had a weird feeling inside of me and felt like my dream had been so real. From that moment on, I knew that I had to do everything in my power to get my life back on track. Giving up just wasn't an option.

I'm sharing this story because some of you

may find yourself in a place where you need help that no one around you can provide. Anxiety and depression following a traumatic life event are both very common. According to the National Institute of Mental Health, approximately 18 percent of adults age eighteen and older will suffer from an anxiety problem in a given year. That's about 40 million people with anxiety! In addition, the National Institutes of Health cites in a 2005 study that approximately 20.9 million American adults or 9.5 percent of the population suffer from mood disorders. This includes not only major depressive disorders, but also chronic mild depression and bipolar disorder. If you find yourself feeling very anxious and/or depressed or are experiencing panic attacks, please do yourself a favor and seek professional help. *(For the warning signs of anxiety and depression, see Figures 1, 2, and 3 on pages 34–36.)*

Figure 1: Warning Signs of Depression

- Persistently feeling sad, anxious, or empty
- Feeling hopeless or pessimistic
- Feeling guilty, worthless, or helpless
- Feeling irritable or restless
- Losing interest in activities or hobbies once pleasurable, including sex
- Experiencing fatigue and decreased energy
- Having trouble concentrating, remembering details, and making decisions
- Experiencing insomnia, early-morning wakefulness, or excessive sleeping
- Overeating or losing your appetite
- Thoughts of suicide, suicide attempts
- Having aches or pains, headaches, cramps, or digestive problems that do not ease even with treatment

Source: National Institute of Mental Health

Figure 2: Warning Signs of Generalized Anxiety Disorder

- Worrying a lot about everyday things
- Having trouble controlling your constant worries
- Knowing that you worry much more than you should
- Being unable to relax
- Having difficulty concentrating
- Being easily startled
- Having trouble falling asleep or staying asleep
- Feeling tired all the time
- Suffering from headaches, muscle aches, stomachaches, or unexplained pains
- Having a hard time swallowing
- Trembling or twitching
- Being irritable
- Sweating a lot
- Feeling light-headed or out of breath
- Frequent urination

Source: National Institute of Mental Health

Figure 3: Warning Signs of Panic Disorder

- Sudden and repeated attacks of fear and panic
- A feeling of being out of control during a panic attack
- An intense worry about when the next attack will happen
- A fear or avoidance of places where panic attacks have occurred in the past
- Physical symptoms, such as a pounding or racing heart, sweating, breathing problems, weakness or dizziness, feeling hot or a cold chill, tingling or numbness in the hands, chest pain, or stomach pain

Source: National Institute of Mental Health

It's always better to seek help as soon as possible because often anxiety problems and depression get worse over time without treatment. This is what happened to me. I kept telling myself I could handle everything on my own. I expected that I could resolve my feelings without any outside help, but in reality the longer I waited, the more severe my anxiety became. It's like I was falling deeper and deeper into a pit. As you can imagine, this was a very dark time in my life. But like all storms, the pain does eventually pass. The emotional pain you are feeling after losing a baby will subside with time, sometimes on its own and other times with some assistance. It is important to remember to always pay attention to both your mind and body. You need to know your limits and recognize when you are having difficulty handling things on your own. I reached a point in my life where there was no doubt it was time for me to figure out what I needed to heal and move on. It was time for me to ask for the help I needed to get my life back. And that is exactly what I did.

"The strong individual is the one
who asks for help when he needs it."
—Rona Barrett, columnist and businesswoman

CHAPTER 3: THE COURAGE TO ASK FOR HELP

Sometimes your problems are just unable to be solved alone. Sometimes your friends and family cannot help or give you what you need. After suffering with severe anxiety and depression for several months, I realized I just could not get through this without some help. My thoughts and emotions were just too powerful and overwhelming for me. Although I preferred to tackle problems myself and never liked to ask anyone for help, I made the difficult decision to seek therapy. After all, I had plenty to work through—the loss of my baby, the ambulance and hospital experience, my fears for my own health, and, of course, the anxiety of it all.

Seeking help, if necessary, is a very important part of the healing process following a loss. No matter how scared you feel or how hard it is to take that first step, you will be thankful you did. It's easy to let pride get in the way or to want to handle your problems all on your own. And you might view seeking help as a sign of weakness or worry that others will see you this way. The truth is that seeking therapy is a sign of strength. It takes a lot of courage to ask for help. It certainly isn't easy to take that first step, but sometimes it's vital for your own emotional well-being. You don't need to suffer. Having a miscarriage is painful enough. You have been through enough and deserve to feel better, to heal and move on. If that means asking for a little assistance, then so be it.

I'm not saying that therapy will be easy or will offer a quick fix. It certainly wasn't easy for me. In fact, going there for the first time is one of the most difficult parts of the process. I remember sitting in the waiting room of the therapy office the first day. I felt so anxious I could hardly sit still. My heart was pounding rapidly in my chest. I felt like if I sat there another minute, I would just jump out of my skin. I was afraid of therapy and what it might entail. I feared the therapist would tell me I was crazy or want to lock me up. I didn't want to be there. I just wanted to run screaming from the building and never come back. But instead I sat and waited and hoped that this person could help me.

Much to my surprise, a friendly, bubbly lady came out to greet me. She looked to be in her sixties, with long, curly blond hair and kind blue eyes. She was comfortably dressed in twill pants and a knit shirt. "Hi, sweetie!" she said enthusiastically and waved for me to come on back.

She was not at all how I pictured a therapist to be. I had a vision in my mind of a businesslike person wearing a skirt suit and looking very educated and serious. This woman, whose name was Judy, was very casual and down to earth. She led me back to her office, which was decorated with bright colors and stuffed animals, and had me sit down on a couch. She asked me to tell her why I was there. I explained to her about the miscarriage, medical scares, panic attacks, and anxiety. I told her I was concerned I was going crazy. She told me right away that I wasn't crazy and that panic attacks and anxiety are very common. She said that the loss of my baby and the medical stuff I went through had triggered them. She was patient, understanding, and encouraging. She reminded me of a mother figure, and I felt at ease telling her my story and sharing my feelings. After meeting with her, I felt somewhat reassured that I could get back to normal again.

In the weeks that followed, I learned more about myself and the source of my problems. It turns out there were many more issues contributing to my anxiety than just my current situation. For one, I had been in an abusive relationship as a teenager and that was affecting my life still. Because of what my ex-boyfriend had done to me, I lacked self-confidence, had difficulty trusting people, and questioned my ability to take care of myself. In addition, I had still not dealt with my feelings surrounding the sudden and unexpected death of my grandfather the year before. He had gone into the hospital for minor outpatient surgery and ended up with septicemia, a serious infection in the blood. The infection affected his heart, and within just a day, he passed away. My whole family was in a state of shock. It didn't seem fair that he was taken so abruptly from us. This experience left me angry with God and questioning my faith.

Along with these issues, I was also a perfectionist and a people pleaser. I spent my life being very hard on myself and disappointed when I didn't live up to my high expectations. I also never liked to let anyone down and would often put everyone else's needs before my own.

Then there was my upbringing. I have a terrific, loving family, but my parents worried a lot and were always overprotective. The sheltered life I led growing up left me unprepared to deal with the challenges of adulthood. I was used to someone always being there to shield me from the bad aspects of life and protect me from harm. Now, I found there were times when my parents were unable to help me deal with some issues because they had never experienced them themselves. No one in my family had ever lost a baby to miscarriage. They were sad and disappointed for me, but they did not know my pain. They didn't have any idea of what to say or do to help. They couldn't possibility understand because they didn't know what it felt like.

For those of you who have miscarried, you know the pain. It is a loss similar to losing a loved one, so you will grieve in much the same way. This, of course, takes time. And, as I've learned, it's important to give yourself all the time you need to grieve and eventually accept what has happened. Don't ever let anyone tell you to just get over it or move on. Grief has no set timetable and is different for each person. Acknowledge and accept your feelings. You have every right to feel sad. Most importantly, seek help if you find yourself overcome by your grief, anxiety, or depression.

My decision to seek help was definitely the best one I made. Little by little, my therapist helped bring out the pains of the past, so that I could resolve them and move on. It was hard work, and I didn't immediately get better. In fact, in the beginning of my therapy, I became even more anxious and began having more intense panic attacks. I worried that therapy was making me worse. When I mentioned this, my therapist told me not to be concerned. She said that happens when you uncover old wounds and try to deal with them. This gets better with time, as you resolve issues and come to terms with what has happened.

Even so, it was difficult to feel worse. I never imagined my anxiety could actually escalate because it had seemed so overwhelming to begin with. Now, it was even harder to function and get through the day. I was doing on-site freelance work as a copy editor at the time. I really don't know how I was able to work at all. One day, my anxiety got so bad, I had to have my husband come and pick me up. Not only was I unable to focus on my work, but I was also unable to drive myself home. I was so relieved when my assignment with that company finally ended.

My difficulty functioning extended beyond my work environment. I also found it nearly impossible to go places and do things I once enjoyed. One time, I panicked in a movie theater, which is supposed to be a relaxing and entertaining place. While trying to watch the movie, I became filled with an overwhelming feeling of fear. I felt the warm rush of blood to my face, my heart began to race, and I suddenly felt trapped in a crowd of people. My breathing became erratic, and my hands began to tingle from hyperventilating. I felt like I needed to escape. I was afraid something bad was going to happen to me. The longer I sat there in the movie theater, the worse I felt. I also worried that other people in the theater would notice my symptoms and think I was strange. I feared being judged and not accepted by others. Looking back, I doubt anyone could tell anything was going on, since I was adept at hiding my feelings from the outside world. Nonetheless, I was unable to get a handle on my anxiety, so we had to leave in the middle of the movie. Once we left the theater, my panic subsided and then the feelings of failure set in.

Although I convinced myself that the movie, *Cookie's Fortune*, wasn't very interesting anyway, I was still angry and disappointed with myself for not being able to stay. Part of anxiety comes from being very hard on yourself and trying to bury your emotions instead of confronting and dealing with them. Negative self-talk also contributes. I was unfortunately accustomed to doing all of these things, which only fueled the anxiety.

The other thing about anxiety is that it can pop up anywhere, at any time, without any warning. It doesn't just happen in dangerous and stressful situations. It's actually quite the opposite. Panic attacks often occur during harmless activities and in safe places, when there really is no logical reason to be afraid or to feel threatened. In addition, panic attacks often happen *after* being in a stressful situation. The danger is gone, but you still react. It's kind of like post-traumatic stress disorder, where patients relive distressing experiences over and over again, especially when something triggers the disturbing memories. This also means that panic can occur in places where you previously had an attack because you relive the experience when you visit that particular location again. Of course, this makes it difficult to function and makes going places and doing normal activities a real challenge.

In my case, anxiety definitely interfered with my normal activities. I panicked in restaurants, malls, and shopping centers. I panicked in the safety of my own home. I even panicked on vacation. One time, my husband and I tried to take a much-needed vacation to Mackinac Island. On the way, we spent one night alone at my parents' cottage near Harrison, Michigan. That night I had intense heart palpitations that lasted for several hours. I checked my pulse at one point and was terrified to find that my heart was beating irregularly. It was skipping beats left and right. My anxiety was so debilitating that we had to turn around and head back home. As a result, my family doctor prescribed Xanax, which is a mild tranquilizer, and my therapist encouraged me to take it daily for a few months to help take the edge off my anxiety. She said I really needed the medication and that it would only be temporary until I was feeling better. I never liked to take medication of any kind, not even aspirin or Tylenol, but I trusted her judgment and wanted to get better, so I agreed to give it a try.

I found that the Xanax did work. It helped lessen the anxiety but did not prevent panic attacks. It made bad days more bearable. Since my anxiety was so intense, I welcomed the chance to feel even a little bit better. After all I had been through, I couldn't argue with the fact that I couldn't continue feeling so horrible. I needed some relief.

The downside was that the medication wore off quickly, leaving me feeling more anxious every morning until I took another pill. After approximately three months on it, I was feeling stronger and decided to quit cold turkey. Big mistake. I had strange buzzing sensations in my head and felt like electricity was running through my entire body. I felt very edgy and could hardly sit still. After consulting with a doctor, I found that I had become dependent on the medication. In my mind, I thought that this must be how people get hooked on drugs. They take something that makes them feel better and then when they decide to stop, they experience uncomfortable symptoms that lead them to take more. Luckily, I was strong enough and smart enough not to stay on the medication any longer than absolutely necessary. I slowly weaned myself off the Xanax over the course of three more months and vowed to never take addictive medication on a daily basis.

I do believe that medication has its place and is sometimes necessary. If you are prescribed medication for depression or anxiety, it is important to remember to take it as directed and never stop abruptly. Many of these drugs have unpleasant side effects and can be harmful if you don't slowly wean yourself off them. Of course, it is always best to go without medication if you're able. Unfortunately, some people don't have this option because they suffer from chemical imbalances in their brains that can only be corrected with medication.

If you're one of the lucky ones who doesn't need medicine to get better, there are some very useful and effective strategies for dealing with depression, grief, and anxiety. One of them is the power that exists within your own mind and heart, as you will continue to discover throughout this book. You will see the various tools I used to deal with my feelings and to eventually have the child I wanted. They worked wonders for me, and I believe they can help you too. The key is to let out your feelings in any way you can. Don't keep them bottled up inside of you. Express yourself. Trust yourself. Have faith. Know that the answers you seek actually already exist inside of you. You just need to find them. I know that sounds easier said that done, but it is true. With time and effort, you can work through a difficult situation and find the resolution you seek.

"There are no good-byes for us.
Wherever you are, you will always be in my heart."
—*Mahatma Gandhi*

CHAPTER 4: SAYING GOOD-BYE

Many things happen during the grieving process as your mind tries to come to terms with what has happened to you. Dealing with the loss of a baby isn't easy, but with time and effort, healing will begin. You'll find that everything you experience has a place and a purpose in your recovery. In my case, I experienced very vivid dreams. They provided some insight into what I was feeling and what I needed to do. In fact, one dream I had actually gave me exactly what I needed to help myself heal. It came as a big surprise to me, and to this day, I still view it as unexpected and miraculous. Here is what happened.

While I was undergoing therapy, I was still

going through a difficult time and continued to have anxiety, panic attacks, and depression for several months following my loss. I was an emotional wreck and was unable to let go of what had happened. I was so completely and totally devastated that I didn't know if I would ever recover. Then one night I fell asleep and an astonishing thing happened. In my dreams, God brought my precious baby to me. He said I could only have one day with her, but he wanted me to have a chance to meet her and care for her before I said good-bye. He felt it was important for me to have some closure and experience a glimpse of motherhood. God handed me my sweet baby girl, and I was immediately filled with an overwhelming sense of love and peace.

That night I held her, fed her, changed her, and rocked her. I kissed her tiny, soft cheek and told her how much I loved her. I did all of the things a new mom would do. It all felt so very real, and I was so happy to finally meet my child. She was the most beautiful baby I had ever seen. She had brown hair and brown eyes and radiant glowing skin. I experienced an amazing, indescribable joy when I was with her.

After I had some time with my baby, God returned and told me it was time to say good-bye. Feelings of sadness came over me, and I naturally cried for my daughter. I didn't want her to go, but I knew I had no choice. I reluctantly handed her over to God, and he disappeared with my child. I woke up with a very unusual feeling, like I had just actually spent time with my baby. I felt calmer and more at ease with my loss. The dream felt so powerful and real to me. It was very healing.

I don't know if this was just a dream that my own mind had created or some sort of divine intervention. The truth is: it really doesn't matter. The important thing is that the dream was a turning point in my recovery. I needed closure. I needed to say good-bye to my child. But since she was not physically present, I was unable to do that. There was no funeral, no burial, and no grave. I had lost a baby, but everything seemed unresolved. One of the hardest parts of suffering a miscarriage is that you usually don't get a chance to see, meet, or hold your baby. She just vanishes from your life as if she never existed. But you and I know that your baby was alive and growing inside of you. She was real and will always be in your heart. No one can ever take that away from you. Your love for your unborn child doesn't just go away when you miscarry. You have a right to grieve. You deserve to have closure.

In my case, I was lucky enough to have an incredible dream that provided me an opportunity to say good-bye to my child in a very special way. After the dream, I felt different. I no longer felt unsettled. I no longer felt like I had never gotten to see or hold my baby. I felt more at peace with what had happened. And that helped me move on with my life.

When you are dealing with the loss of a baby, my best advice is to do whatever you can to find closure. You may not be able to meet your baby or say good-bye in a dream. But there are many other things you can do that will help. Whether it's planting a flower, writing a poem or letter to your child, or lighting a candle at church, you need to say good-bye and acknowledge your loss in some way. This is a crucial part of the healing process. No matter how you are feeling, taking the time to do something to honor the baby you lost can only benefit you in the long run.

I'll never forget the day I planted a peach-colored rosebush for my baby. I miscarried at the end of April and purchased the rosebush sometime in late May. My dad was with me. He dug a hole in the ground on the side of the brick ranch my husband and I shared in Sterling Heights, Michigan. It was our first home, and I had looked forward to starting a family there. I remember it was a beautiful, sunny spring day. The sky was bright blue and filled with fluffy white clouds. There was a warm, gentle breeze. I recall thinking that I should be enjoying such a gorgeous day, but I wasn't. After I placed the rosebush in the ground and gently patted the soil around it, I stood up just staring at it. Life did not seem fair. I was so lost and numb and alone. Even in the company of my helpful and supportive father, I felt like there was no one there but me. I was in a fog, unable to feel much of anything. It didn't matter what the weather was doing outside. On the inside, I was filled with a dark, gray storm cloud. There was no light, no breeze, and no sound. All I could think was, "This is all I have left to remember my baby."

What I didn't realize that day is that the

rosebush would later become an important symbol for me. It would become a sign of hope for the future. The rosebush was a reminder that life goes on. Memories live forever, and new ones are created each day. Even in your darkest hour, there is always hope. You just need to open your heart and mind to what awaits. I didn't know it at the time, but there was so much more in store for me. My life wasn't over; it was just beginning.

"What lies behind us and what lies before us
are tiny matters compared to what lies within us."
—Ralph Waldo Emerson

CHAPTER 5: STRENGTH RENEWED

As I continued with my therapy, my strength returned more and more each week. I shed a lot of tears and talked about my worse fears, hurts of the past, and insecurities. At home, I also did several things that helped me heal. I planted colorful flowers in front of our house. I wrote my feelings in a journal. I went for walks outside. Whenever I was feeling down or discouraged, I would remind myself of everything I had to be thankful for and make a list. My list included simple things like: my family, the birds nesting on our porch light, the way the trees sway gently in the wind, a sunset, the beach, the beautiful spring weather, and the flowers that were in full bloom.

Reminding yourself of the blessings in your life can really help put things in perspective.

After several months of therapy, I began to return to normal. One day I realized I was laughing and talking to my therapist about everyday things. I had nothing left to uncover. I had finally healed. The therapist told me it was a pleasure working with me and gave me a hug. She said she was proud of the work I had done and the progress I had made. With tears in my eyes, I said good-bye, all the while wondering if I was really ready to make it on my own again.

It turns out I was. Shortly after leaving therapy, I landed a great job as a publications editor at Kmart's corporate headquarters. I had my own office, an awesome boss and coworkers, and a lot of freedom. I was able to redesign the company newsletter and implement changes to the content. My superiors were very receptive to my ideas and trusted my judgment. I loved my job and was thrilled to use my creativity. And I met some great friends at work, some of whom I am still in touch with today.

I continued to grow and thrive each day. I was not only living again, but also open to new experiences. I flew on an airplane for the first time—something I had always been terrified to do. Our friends, Don and Michelle, who lived in Knoxville, Tennessee, invited us to meet them in Las Vegas. I was uncertain of whether or not I could go through with the trip and had actually decided I was too afraid. I'll never forget the day

Michelle called me at work to see what I had decided. I was all prepared to say no, but when she asked me, my reply was, "I think I'd like to try it." I shocked myself and had no idea where those words had come from. I guess deep down I knew I was strong enough and ready to fly. And I certainly was! It turns out flying was far less scary than I had imagined it to be. I even thought looking out the window during takeoff and landing was cool. And I was so excited to see the Rocky Mountains from up above. I was also thrilled to be able to take some amazing pictures of the mountains and clouds from the plane window. It was an incredible view!

After that, I continued to become stronger. My confidence increased, and I was no longer afraid of life. No one would have ever guessed the grief and anxiety I had been through after my miscarriage. I had transformed back into a well-adjusted, happy person. I flew two other times—once to New Orleans for a wedding and another to San Francisco for our ten-year wedding anniversary. I took piano lessons and joined a hip-hop dance class—two things I had always wanted to do. I joined Jazzercise, a fitness class that combines dance with exercise and weight training. I was feeling strong, healthy, vibrant, and in control of my life. It felt great to once again enjoy life!

My point to all this is: no matter how you are feeling after losing a baby, you will get through it, and you will enjoy your life again. The tears dry. The pain lessens. And one day you start to feel yourself again. This does not mean you ever forget what happened or that you stop longing for a child. I still remember the date I first miscarried—April 30, 1999. That date will be forever burned in my mind. It is a significant part of my history and my journey to become a parent. It shaped me into the person I am today and ultimately led me to my daughter. As I mentioned, I never for one moment stopped longing to be a mom. Even though I was doing really well and enjoying my life again, there was still one thing missing. I knew my life would not be complete until I was a mother. But after what I went through with the first pregnancy, I was understandably afraid to try again. So I decided to put parenthood on hold for a while until I felt ready and found the courage to give it another try.

I believe it's important to give yourself all the time you need until you are emotionally prepared to attempt another pregnancy. For some, this may come in a matter of months. You may be eager to become pregnant again right away and continue your journey to parenthood without much interruption. For others, it may take years before you are ready. And that is okay. You will know when and if the time is right.

Following my miscarriage and therapy, I continued to work full-time and spend time with my family and friends. The rosebush I had planted to honor the baby we lost grew and flourished. Every time I would look at it, it reminded me of our child. I kept thinking how ironic it was that our baby didn't make it, but the rose was thriving. It was almost as if the love I had for my unborn child was thriving too, that a part of her was still living on even though she couldn't be with me. I saw the rose as a sign of hope. On Valentine's Day, nearly two years after my miscarriage, I felt inspired to write a poem about the baby we lost and the rose that was left behind in her place. This is what I wrote.

The Precious Rose

From love's sweet embrace
She was created
Destined for greater things
And as we awaited her arrival
A storm brewed within
Threatening to take her
From those closest to her heart
Tender rose petals
Shed from the stem that once gave life
Dreams dissolved
Hope shattered
But the rose remains

(—Deanna Kahler, 2/14/2001)

Writing is definitely a great outlet for your emotions. Keeping a journal or writing a poem does wonders to help you deal with your loss and sort out your feelings. Don't worry if you're not a writer. That doesn't matter. What matters is that you release what is inside of you and express your innermost feelings and thoughts. No one ever has to read what you write. It is just for you. You don't need to concern yourself with grammar or style. All you need to do is pick up a pen and write what is on your mind and in your heart. To help get started, ask yourself some questions. How are you feeling? Are you angry, sad, frustrated, confused, or numb? What are your concerns, worries, and fears? What are your hopes for the future? Write whatever comes to mind, even if your thoughts are scattered. Get it all down on paper. Then, when you are finished reread it.

I've found that once I finish writing, my problems and concerns make more sense to me. Everything becomes clearer. I understand myself better. Sometimes I even find solutions to problems after writing out my feelings and reading what I wrote. It's a sort of cleansing of the mind. Once you clear out the thoughts and feelings that are troubling you, there is room for reflection and for pondering what to do next. Writing is such an invaluable tool for healing. And, after a miscarriage, there is much healing that is needed. Only when you have resolved your feelings and dealt with your loss can you move on with your life.

Sometimes during the healing process, the unexpected happens. As your mind becomes clearer, you're more open to noticing and experiencing life's mysterious gifts. You're no longer consumed with grief or fear and are able to receive the positive energy that is all around you. It is at this point that miracles can occur. And sometimes something comes into your life at the right time, allowing you to learn and prepare for what's next. That is what happened to me.

"To believe in the things you can see and touch is no belief at all; but to believe in the unseen is a triumph and a blessing."
—Abraham Lincoln

CHAPTER 6: WE MET IN A DREAM

About two years after my miscarriage, I was still doing really well. I thought about trying to have a baby again, but the timing just didn't feel right to me. My life was really good, and I wasn't ready to "rock the boat." Even so, I imagined what it would be like to be a mom quite often and knew that one day I needed to make it happen.

Then one night I had a dream about a baby girl. Her name was Ashley, and she had brown hair and brown eyes. I was helping my mom take care of her in the family room at my parents' house. I felt a strong connection to this baby, but I knew I wasn't her mother. In my dream, I didn't know whose baby she was, only that I was related to her in some way. It was such a powerful dream. My emotions and my experiences with this child seemed so very real and so touching.

I woke up a little puzzled and thought the dream was interesting. What did it mean? Naturally, my inquisitive and analytical mind tried to make sense of it. I concluded that I must have had the dream because I still wanted to be a mom so badly and didn't know if it would happen to me. So I allowed myself the opportunity to care for a child who wasn't mine, enjoying the experience, yet knowing that she was someone else's daughter. I don't know where the name Ashley came from, since it wasn't one of the names I had chosen or even considered for our child. But I didn't think much of it. Dreams are like that. Sometimes you just don't know how you came up with the details. Little did I know, this dream was far more significant than I could have ever imagined. It wasn't until a few months later that I realized what it all meant.

I was sitting on the couch with my sister Dawn at her house. We were talking when she handed me a picture of an ultrasound. "This is your niece or nephew," she smiled. I was surprised because I had no idea my sister and her husband were even trying to have a baby. As I looked at the tiny picture of the growing baby, I felt both happy and envious. This was my "little" sister, and a part of me felt like I was supposed to have a baby first. I was the one who should have given my parents their first grandchild. But life doesn't always work out the way you plan. Even though I was disappointed and sad for myself, I still couldn't help but be excited for Dawn. My sister was going to have a baby! She was going to be a mom! This was a big, important moment in her life—one that many women dream of. I congratulated her and gave her a hug.

"Do you have any names picked out?" I asked.

"If it's a girl, our top name choice is Ashley," she replied.

A weird tingly sensation came over me and chills ran down my spine. If I wasn't sitting, I very well may have fallen down on the floor at that moment. My mind instantly flashed back to the unusual dream I had months earlier. A baby girl named Ashley! I suddenly felt like I was in an episode of *The Twilight Zone.* The baby I dreamed about must have been my sister's unborn child. The whole thing was so bizarre to me. I had somehow received knowledge of a future event. My dream was a precognition! How was this even possible?

Throughout my sister's pregnancy, everyone—including her—was convinced she was having a boy. They all had their reasons: the way her stomach was shaped, which foods she craved, etc. But I knew better. I firmly believed all along that she would have a girl. That girl would be Ashley, the baby in my dream. There was no doubt in my mind about this.

When my sister did finally deliver the baby, her child was, in fact, a girl. She had brown hair and brown eyes. And they did name her Ashley! The whole experience was just so bizarre. I saw something in my dream that I just couldn't possibly have known. I questioned why I was given this knowledge ahead of time. After a lot of thinking, I finally decided it must be because I am supposed to have a strong connection to this baby. When I met Ashley for the first time in person, my theory was confirmed.

I remember walking in the hospital room shortly after the delivery. My brother-in-law Tom was holding and rocking Ashley, tears streaming down his face. It was the most touching and beautiful moment I had ever witnessed. I was filled with an overwhelming joy, and my own eyes brimmed with tears. As I looked at baby Ashley, she blinked softly and her beautiful long eyelashes fluttered like a delicate butterfly. She was so alert, taking in all of her surroundings and studying the people near her. She was the most precious child I had ever met. I immediately felt a strong connection to her. This child was special to me. Maybe because our bond had begun before she even existed.

In the months that followed, my bond with my new niece strengthened. I had the honor of becoming her godmother. I babysat her often and spent as much time with her as I could. When she was upset, I rocked her to sleep humming the tune from the game show *Jeopardy*. From some reason, I discovered that the song really calmed her down. She also liked "Ashley Nicole Had a Farm," which, of course, was my version of "Old MacDonald."

Some of you may also have nieces or nephews that you are close to. If you do, then you know that it is wonderful to have a special child in your life. It's also a fantastic feeling to play a role in teaching, nurturing, and shaping that child. And it's exciting to watch him or her learn and grow.

Ashley grew quickly and the days passed. Soon she became old enough to talk and for some reason decided to call me "Ba." When I came to visit, she would squeal with delight and run to the door shouting, "Ba Ba Ba!" It gave me such a great feeling inside to be so cherished and loved by a child. Ashley was also very intelligent and inquisitive. She didn't miss anything and was constantly scanning her environment and trying to learn all she could. She had such a quest for knowledge unlike anything I had ever seen. I recall carrying her around the house as she pointed at everything asking "Dat?" which was her way of saying, "What's that?" I was always happy to teach her and help explain the world around her.

My niece was like a daughter to me, and I am so grateful to my sister for allowing me the marvelous opportunity to become close to her and experience some of the joys that parents do. I was thrilled to be able to accompany Ashley, my sister, and her husband Tom to the beach, park, zoo, and mall. My husband and I also took a trip to Washington, DC, with them when my niece was just two years old.

There's no doubt that having a special niece or nephew in your life is a blessing. But as much as you love and enjoy that child, it is never a substitute for having a baby of your own to love and care for.

As hard as you try, you can't actually experience motherhood until you *become* a mom.

This all became clear to me one day when I was babysitting Ashley at my house. We were playing on the great room floor near the couch. As I watched my niece, I became filled with a sad longing. I loved Ashley dearly, but I ached for a child of my own. Many of you can relate to this longing. It's that feeling inside that a part of you is missing or incomplete. You need something more to make you feel whole.

Sensing my sadness, Ashley looked up at me and said, "Aunt Deanna, I love you."

"I love you too!" I replied.

Then she repeated with more emphasis, "I love you! I love you! *I love you!*"

I couldn't help but smile. My sweet little niece knew what I needed. She instinctively picked up on my sadness and wanted me to know that it was okay. That she was there for me and she loved me. Bless her little heart!

There was no denying after that moment that it was time for me to work on my own life. It was time to fulfill my own dream of becoming a mom. I had gotten as close as I possibly could to being a mom. I was an aunt and a godmother. I shared a very special bond with my niece. But it wasn't enough for me. As close as we were, Ashley wasn't *my* child. I didn't get to tuck her into bed each night. I didn't get to comfort her when she was sick. I didn't get to wake each morning to her beautiful smiling face. There was definitely something missing in my life. As anyone who longs for a child knows, there is nothing that can make that yearning and aching go away. Nothing except actually becoming a mom. It was time for me to try to make this happen. I was finally ready to give it another shot.

"You gain strength, courage and confidence
by every experience in which you really stop
to look fear in the face.... You must do the thing
that you think you cannot do."
—*Eleanor Roosevelt*

CHAPTER 7: HERE WE GO AGAIN

About four years had passed since my miscarriage. The year was 2003, just two years after my niece was born. Somewhere deep inside of me, I finally found the strength and courage to try to have a baby again. I was thirty-four at the time, and my doctor told me it might take a little longer to conceive because I was getting older. It didn't. Just like the first time my husband and I tried to conceive, I became pregnant within just two months.

When I saw the plus sign on the home pregnancy test, I cried tears of great joy. Again, I was so excited about becoming a mom. This time I bought some maternity clothes, anticipating that I would actually need them. My husband was also really ready to be a dad and was far less fearful than with the first pregnancy. It was refreshing to see his excitement and anticipation. I'll never forget the night he said he loved me and then added to my stomach, "I love you too, baby." It was one of the sweetest things I had ever heard. My heart just melted.

Shortly after finding out I was pregnant, I visited my OB/GYN who ran blood tests right away and found that the clotting antibodies were no longer present. She also tested my pregnancy hormone levels, otherwise known as human chorionic gonadotropin (hCG). They were strong and at the appropriate level for the stage of my pregnancy. My doctor said I didn't need to take aspirin or do Heparin injections. All looked promising, and she was very optimistic about a positive outcome this time. It was so reassuring to hear the good news! I felt hopeful and relieved.

There were many other positive indicators as well. For one, this time my pregnancy felt different. Unlike with my first pregnancy, I had strong food cravings for beef, Mexican dishes, and lemon-flavored sweets. I felt nauseous, especially in the morning. I had hot flashes. I was tired all the time. I had terrible heartburn. And, I had aching, swollen breasts. It looked like I was experiencing a pretty normal pregnancy. All the right signs were there. All was well.

Nearly ten weeks of my pregnancy passed, and it was almost time for my long-awaited appointment to hear the baby's heartbeat. I knew once I heard this glorious sound that I would be far less likely to miscarry. According to the American Pregnancy Association, once a fetal heartbeat is detected, the chances of the pregnancy continuing range from 70 to 90 percent. I eagerly awaited this day, hoping and praying that this time our baby would be okay. This time, I would have a normal pregnancy and deliver a healthy child.

Then one day I started to feel less pregnant. I couldn't explain it, but my body felt different in some way. Maybe it was that my intense food cravings had diminished. Or maybe it was that I didn't feel so queasy anymore. Or that my breasts didn't feel so sore. Whatever the case, I felt like something was amiss. I tried to convince myself that I was just nervous because I had miscarried once before. But deep inside of me, something just didn't feel right.

That night I had a dream about my sister. I dreamed I took her to the doctor because she was bleeding. The doctor said my sister was having a miscarriage and that the baby had stopped developing at five weeks and five days. I awoke from my dream with my heart pounding and a sense of impending doom. I felt scared and sad. I immediately woke up my husband.

"I think the baby's dead!" I cried.

He seemed shocked by my words and assured me that I was just worrying because of the last miscarriage. He reminded me that I wasn't bleeding, and there weren't any other signs that I was miscarrying. I told him I didn't feel pregnant anymore. I told him I believed the dream was true, but it was about me. He hugged me tight and dismissed my fears. He told me everything was going to be all right, and he seemed so sure of it. I tried my best to hold on to faith, and I drifted back to sleep.

A couple of days later, it was time for my ten-week appointment. My doctor examined me and then got out the equipment to listen for the baby's heartbeat. I felt my own heart beat quickly as I anticipated the moment. I prayed that my doctor would find the heartbeat and the baby would be fine. Then I lay there on the table listening, waiting, hoping, and praying some more.

My doctor tried for several minutes to detect the baby's heartbeat. She slowly moved the instrument all around and adjusted the volume on the machine. At first, she found my own heartbeat, pounding quickly in anticipation. It sounded like a horse galloping. Although my pulse was fast, it wasn't as fast as it would be for a developing baby at this stage of the pregnancy. My pulse was around 120, where the baby's would be 150 or higher. I was surprised at how fast my heart was beating. But then again, it was understandable. I was so nervous as I awaited the results.

My doctor continued to search for the heartbeat, but was having trouble finding it. The longer it took, the more concerned I became.

Finally, after what seemed like an eternity, my doctor told me she was unable to find the baby's heartbeat. My own heart sank. "It's happening all over again," I thought. She said that didn't mean there was a problem. Sometimes at this stage of the pregnancy the heartbeat is just hard to detect. She ordered an ultrasound, and I headed over to the hospital to learn my baby's fate. A part of me already knew.

At the hospital, the ultrasound technician showed me the developing sac. She said everything looked normal from what she could see; however, she could not see the fetus. She said that according to the test, I was only five weeks pregnant, not ten. At five weeks, the fetus would be too small to see. She was encouraging and suggested that maybe I had miscalculated and wasn't as far along as I had thought. But I knew that was not the case. I was sure the baby had stopped developing at five weeks, just like in my dream. I left the hospital in tears.

Within a couple of days, I began experiencing pain and bleeding. My doctor ordered more blood work to check my pregnancy hormone levels, which were unfortunately declining. I was miscarrying once again. My doctor told me she was very sorry. She said she had high hopes this time because my HCG levels were so strong in the beginning. She ordered more blood work to see if the blood clotting antibodies were back. And I went back to the hospital for another D&C. I had the option of waiting to see if a D&C was necessary, but I didn't want to have any emergencies or severe bleeding like the last time I miscarried. I once again opted for a spinal, instead of general anesthesia. This time I was lucky enough to have my regular doctor, which was a huge comfort to me.

The surgery was much less stressful than the first time. Maybe it was because I had been through it all before or maybe because it wasn't an emergency this time. Whatever the reason, I was stronger and less afraid. As the doctor worked on me, the nurses kept asking if I needed some medication. I continued to refuse. One nurse remarked that I was the only patient he had ever seen that went through the procedure without any pain medication. He was amazed at how well I did being totally alert and awake during the surgery. I guess I was strong and brave enough this time to not need any. After all, I had already lived through a miscarriage and D&C. I was a survivor!

After the D&C, my doctor told me she ordered a chromosome analysis on the remnants of my pregnancy to see if there were any genetic abnormalities with the baby. She said this could provide more clues as to why I miscarried again. Sometimes the developing baby has too many or two few chromosomes. Or there may be defects in the chromosomes themselves. This could result in the fetus not being viable. I thanked my doctor for her help and was then taken to recovery. This time, they gave me my own private room and served me a spaghetti dinner because I was starving. I ate almost all of it and was very eager to go home.

Since I was numb from the waist down and couldn't move my legs or feet, I had to wait. Every time the nurse would come in to check on me, I tried with all my might to wiggle my toes, and I rocked my body back and forth in an attempt to get my legs working again. Although it still took a couple of hours for the spinal to wear off, the nurses were amazed at how soon I was standing and ready to go home. They remarked what a trooper I was through all of it.

While I was in recovery, my mom came in to see me. I think in some ways she felt guilty for not being there during my heart-attack scare after my first miscarriage. I must admit I was hard on her back then and not very understanding. For a long time, I didn't forgive her for not being there. This time things were different. I knew how much my mom loved me. And I understood that my pain was her pain too. She had tears in her eyes and said she was sorry for my loss. She had this sorrowful look on her face like she felt really terrible for me. I was sad too, but my strength and confidence were fully intact this time. I looked her straight in the eyes and said firmly and with determination, "It's not over. I will have a baby one day!"

I wasn't sure how or when it would happen, but I believed with all my heart that this was true. That belief is what carries you through the tough times and gives you the will to do everything in your power to make your dreams come true. No matter how bleak things may seem at the time, there is always hope and always a way to make something happen. I was driven to make my dreams a reality! I just had to figure out how.

A few days later the results of my tests were in. I remember I was having a garage sale when the phone rang. A friend and former neighbor was with me, and I had explained to her that if the abnormal clotting antibodies were present once again, that I would most likely not pursue a third pregnancy. Two losses were enough of an emotional upheaval for me. I had no desire to go through that again. Also, I was not comfortable with the idea of injecting myself with blood thinners and the risks involved during pregnancy. I was hoping the doctor would give me good news, but I was somewhat prepared for what she might say.

My doctor told me that I again tested positive for anticardiolipin antibodies. However, unlike my first miscarriage, the test for the lupus anticoagulant came back abnormal as well. Both anticardiolipin antibodies and the lupus anticoagulant belong to a group called antiphospholipid antibodies, which are directed against phospholipid-binding plasma proteins. In simple terms, as I mentioned before, autoantibodies mistake healthy cells for foreign invaders and attack them, in much the same way your immune system would attack a cold virus or bacterial infection. There are approximately twenty different types of antiphospholipid antibodies, but they all have a similar effect: an increased risk of blood clots, heart attacks, and strokes. Approximately 15 percent of women with recurrent miscarriages persistently test positive for either anticardiolipin antibodies or the lupus anticoagulant. Most miscarriages in women with these antibodies occur between weeks seven and twelve of the pregnancy, and chromosome analysis reveals that the fetuses were normal. This was the case with my loss.

My doctor informed me that the chromosome analysis showed a "normal female." A genetic problem was most likely not the cause of my miscarriage. Was the fact that my baby was normal supposed to make me feel better? It certainly didn't. I became fixated on the word *female*. All I could think about was the fact that the baby was a girl, just like I had always wanted. There was nothing physically wrong with her. The problem was with me and my body, specifically my blood.

After I got off the phone, I didn't say a word and just burst into tears. My friend gave me a hug and an understanding look. She knew what it was like to want a baby so badly and have to struggle to have one. Although she hadn't suffered a miscarriage, she had experienced some infertility issues and received treatment in order to have her kids. She was familiar with the longing, the waiting, and the disappointment. Like me, she had considered adoption. I was glad she happened to be there for support when I received the news from my doctor. Otherwise, I would have been all alone in my cold, dark garage. Sometimes the timing of life's events is perfect.

My friend offered a sympathetic ear and a shoulder to cry on. Those things are important when you lose a baby. Understandably, having

DEANNA KAHLER

another miscarriage brought up a wealth of emotions and feelings of guilt once again. Even though I knew I didn't cause my miscarriage, I once again felt somehow responsible. My baby didn't grow and develop normally because my body didn't do what it was supposed to. I also thought because I had tested positive for blood clotting antibodies in the past, that I should have known better than to expect I could have a normal pregnancy the second time. Did I put my unborn child at risk by even attempting another pregnancy? Should I have taken baby aspirin during my pregnancy?

Despite these thoughts, the fact is that I did everything I was supposed to. I was retested for these antibodies at the beginning of my pregnancy, and they were no longer present. At the time, there was no need to be on blood thinners or receive extra monitoring and care. Everything was normal, so there was really no reason to believe I was in danger of miscarrying again. No one could have anticipated that the antibodies would appear again later in my pregnancy. Once again, it really was no one's fault.

As I mentioned, it is common to feel guilty or blame yourself for a pregnancy loss, but the fact remains: you did nothing to cause it. That, of course, doesn't change the emotions you will experience. I had lost a daughter. I felt sad, angry, and bewildered. I couldn't believe this was happening to me a second time. I was determined to ensure that this never happened again.

In light of my second batch of abnormal tests,

76

my doctor suggested I see a rheumatologist and perinatologist once again. Within a couple of weeks, my husband and I headed back to Henry Ford Hospital in downtown Detroit to meet with a perinatologist. As I sat across from the doctor, she told me I was lucky. She said that she had seen other women with these blood clotting antibodies who had life-threatening problems and catastrophic organ failure. She explained that clots can form anywhere in your body—even within the organs themselves. Sometimes clots can travel to your heart or brain, which results in a heart attack or stroke. She said that it was encouraging news that I had never had any clots and that my only problem was the miscarriages. Somehow, that didn't make me feel reassured or lucky.

After visiting with the perinatologist and a rheumatologist, along with having a host of additional blood tests, doctors concluded I most likely had antiphospholipid syndrome. This chronic lifelong condition can cause many health problems, with the most common being recurrent pregnancy loss. In fact, women who have it have about a 90 to 95 percent chance of miscarrying. The treatment is baby aspirin along with self-administered, twice-daily injections of Heparin into your stomach throughout the pregnancy. The two medications combined increase the live birth rate for future pregnancies to around 70 percent or more. But the treatment doesn't come without risks. There is a high complication rate among women who are treated with these medications during pregnancy.

Some of the problems encountered include: gestational hypertension, antepartum hemorrhage, premature birth, and small birth-weight babies. As I mentioned before, I was not comfortable with the risks involved and certainly didn't want to inject myself in the stomach every day during my pregnancy, so having a baby the traditional way became nearly impossible for us.

As you can imagine, it was very difficult to accept that my husband and I would not be able to have the child we so desired. I cried, and I grieved once again. I remember heading down the stairs at our house one morning and just collapsing into a sobbing heap halfway down. Soon after, my husband started to head down the stairs to go to work. He stopped suddenly when he saw me. He gave me a sympathetic look and a big hug. I just cried my eyes out and said, "What are we going to do?" Those familiar heart-wrenching feelings of emotional pain and loss had returned. I was once again devastated.

Despite having a second miscarriage, history did not entirely repeat itself. This time, I handled my loss differently. I did not let my feelings consume me. I kept busy. I exercised regularly. I pushed myself to do activities I enjoyed no matter how sad or depressed I felt. I gave myself time to heal, while considering our options and determining the best way for us to have a child. I let my feelings out when I needed to. I did all of the things that helped after my first miscarriage and none of the things that didn't. I also wrote this poem.

Tiny Bud

A tiny bud forms—and life begins
The bud is nurtured
By the warmth of the sun
By the love of its admirers
By the soothing touch of the wind
Yet it is never more than just a bud

It is no less real or beautiful
Than the flower it was supposed to be
But we will never see it grow
Or thrive
Or flourish
We can never smell its sweet scent
Or gently touch its soft petals

But we cannot dismiss it
It is an important part of nature itself
For without that bud, there can be no life
It holds the key
To dreams unrealized
To hopes unfulfilled
And to a promise of better things to come

(—Deanna Kahler, 2003)

I can't stress enough the importance of keeping busy no matter how terrible you feel. The more normal activities you do, the more normal you will feel. Writing that poem allowed me to express my innermost feelings and say good-bye to my second unborn child. In addition, exercise turned out to be a tremendous release for my emotions. No matter how depressed or sad I felt, I forced myself to exercise. Afterward, I always felt better. Plus, when you keep busy and do activities you enjoy, it helps keep your mind from dwelling on the sadness. So, whether it's writing, exercising, shopping, gardening, or having lunch with a friend, do whatever makes you feel good, even if you don't feel up to it. It will definitely help make it easier to resolve your grief and come up with a plan on how to proceed. I've included a list of tips and suggestions for activities that can be helpful on the next page.

Tips for Easing Grief:

Here is a list of tips you can try to help ease your grief and keep your mind busy.

1) **Get outside and experience nature**. There's something about being outdoors that helps you feel more peaceful, grounded, and connected. It doesn't really matter what you choose to do—gardening, going for a walk, or simply sitting in your yard and listening to the birds. Choose an activity that appeals to you and enjoy some fresh air.

2) **Exercise.** We all know that exercise is a natural mood booster and can help relieve stress, improve sleep patterns, and ease fatigue. Try hiking, running, dancing, bike riding, yoga, aerobics, weight training, Pilates, or any other activity that gets you moving.

3) **Talk to a friend or relative.** Getting your feelings out is always helpful and can be a big release. Confide in someone you trust and share your fears, sorrow, and concerns. They will no doubt offer you a sympathetic ear and some encouraging words.

4) **Pray.** Never underestimate the power of prayer. Even if you aren't religious or don't

attend church, simply asking for support from God or the universe can result in positive changes in your life.

5) **Write out your feelings**. Start a journal where you write about what you are thinking and how you are feeling. Getting the words down on paper and out of your head can be very freeing and often leads to realizations or a change in perspective. If you don't want to write in a journal, try writing a poem or just putting random thoughts and feelings down on paper.

6) **Think of the blessings in your life**. Remember to be grateful for all the marvelous gifts you have in your life. It can be helpful when you're feeling down or discouraged to make a list of everything and everyone you are thankful for. It really helps put things into perspective and can lift your spirits.

7) **Read a good book or magazine.** Pick something to read that is light and fun and will take you away from your worries, concerns, and fears temporarily.

8) **See a funny movie.** We've all heard the phrase "Laughter is the best medicine." Try watching a comedy to improve your mood.

9) **Join a support group**. Sometimes we feel alone in our struggles and think that no one understands. Joining a support group either online or in your local neighborhood can help. You will communicate with others who share the same experiences and who understand how you feel. You will also get additional support and tips from those who have been there and survived.

10) **Volunteer**. Helping others can make us feel useful, worthwhile, and appreciated. Volunteering will also keep you busy and give you something and someone else to focus on.

11) **Plant something to honor the person you lost**. As I mentioned, I planted a rosebush in memory of the first baby I lost. Seeing the roses blooming and growing filled me with love and hope for the future. The flowers were a special reminder of my child. I also made a tree donation in honor of a former boyfriend who passed away. You can have trees planted in a national forest in someone's name. The Arbor Day Foundation and a few other organizations offer this service. Planting a bush, tree, or flower is a special way to honor someone important to you who passed. It is symbolic of the beauty of life and is a reminder that life continues and memories live on.

12) **Take a trip or vacation**. Sometimes a change of scenery and environment is exactly what we need to feel better. It's always nice to get away, especially when your feelings become overwhelming and you need a break.

13) **Start a project.** A project can really help shift your focus and give you sense of empowerment and accomplishment. When someone close to me was diagnosed with cancer and had to move out of state for a couple of months for treatment, I was naturally very upset, worried, and afraid. I couldn't imagine my life without my loved one and felt so powerless over the circumstances. I felt restless and needed to do something to keep busy. So I redecorated a bedroom. I stripped a wallpaper border, painted a stripe, put decals on the wall, and purchased new bedding and a valance. I must admit, ripping wallpaper off the wall was great for stress relief! And seeing the finished project gave me a terrific and proud feeling inside. Redecorating can provide a sense of normalcy, make the time pass faster, and help you worry less and feel in control of something in your life.

14) **Learn something new**. Take a class or learn something you've always wanted to

try. In between my first and second miscarriages, I decided to participate in activities I had always hoped to try, but never had the time for. As I mentioned, I learned to play piano in my thirties. I took an adult hip-hop dance class. I joined a Jazzercise exercise class. These were all great ways to keep me busy and give me something to strive for.

15) **Listen to music.** Music is also great for brightening your mood. Play your favorite songs and dance or sing along. Or if you prefer, choose something more soothing and just lay down and listen.

16) **Try meditation**. There are some fantastic guided mediation CDs that can really help relax you and make you feel more focused and centered. One of my personal favorites is *Your Present: A Half-Hour of Peace* by Susie Mantell.

17) **Let out your frustration.** I know this will probably sound silly or crazy, but if you're feeling really angry or frustrated, just scream. Go into your basement or somewhere where your neighbors won't hear you and let out a big, long scream. I've done this once or twice in my life (when I was home alone, of course) and have been amazed at how much better I felt.

18) **Cry.** In a society where we're often taught to hold in our feelings and hide our emotions, it's easy to forget how healthy it is to just cry when you need to. Letting your feelings out can bring tremendous relief. It's always better to release what's inside of you, instead of keeping your feelings buried where they can resurface later and cause physical or emotional health problems.

"We must be willing to let go of the life we have planned, so as to have the life that is waiting for us."
—*E. M. Forster*

CHAPTER 8: WHERE DO WE GO FROM HERE?

After I gave myself enough time to grieve and heal from my miscarriages, it was time to figure out what was next. When making this decision, the best advice I can offer is to make sure you do what you feel in your heart is right for you. Friends and relatives will offer lots of advice and opinions—they certainly did with me—so try not to be swayed by what others think. Remember that what is right for one person can be very wrong for someone else. Everyone will have a different path, depending on life circumstances. But if you trust your intuition and your inner voice, you will always end up in the right place.

Some women know right away that they must try again. They are very driven to have a baby the traditional way. I've read stories of women who have had four, five, or even more miscarriages, and they still keep trying. It means so much to them to give birth to a child that they just don't give up. Some do eventually succeed; others follow another path after they're satisfied they have done enough. I've never been a quitter, but after the pain and turmoil I experienced following my losses, attempting another pregnancy just wasn't the right choice for me anymore.

Not everyone will feel that way, so if having a baby the traditional way is the choice that feels best for you, then definitely go for it. Just make sure you proceed from a cautious and educated standpoint.

I certainly don't recommend just blindly attempting pregnancy after pregnancy. For one, the emotional turmoil can be very overwhelming. Also, the stress and strain on your body isn't healthy either. And, each time you miscarry, your chances of successfully giving birth drop. According to a *New York Times* article "Trying Again After Recurrent Miscarriages," 80 to 90 percent of women go on to have a successful pregnancy after just one miscarriage. However, after two and three pregnancy losses, this rate drops to 75 percent and 65 percent, respectively. These figures represent women who have not received any form of treatment during their pregnancies. So if you do decide to attempt another pregnancy, it's important to get to the root of the problem, so that you can get the appropriate treatment to increase your chances of success.

If attempting another pregnancy doesn't feel right to you, you definitely have many life choices. Some women decide that they have given themselves enough chances at motherhood and that it isn't meant to be for them. They choose another path that will give them happiness and fulfillment in other ways. They may focus on a new career, travel the world, or take on a new role that incorporates children into their lives. Some women decide to become teachers, nannies, nurses, counselors, or other professionals that work with kids on a daily basis. This gives them a fantastic opportunity to nurture, care for, guide, and make a difference in the lives of many children. It's a great option if you love working with kids and no longer have a burning desire to be a parent.

For many women, however, caring for other people's kids is rewarding, but just not enough. They will not be fulfilled or satisfied until they actually become a parent. If that is the case with you, as it was with me, you *can* find a way to make it happen.

I was determined to become a mother. Somehow, in my heart, adoption felt right all along. I felt drawn to it. Looking back, I realize that I had been unknowingly preparing for adoption my whole life. Certain experiences and situations had appeared beginning in my childhood that would eventually lead me to the path I was meant to take.

The earliest experience I remember is when I

was in elementary school and learned that my best friend was adopted by her stepfather. I recall thinking how wonderful it was that this man had chosen to make his relationship as her father official. I witnessed the tremendous amount of love in that family and thought it was very special. At an early age, it was already obvious to me that biology is not what binds us to others; it is love and the strength of our relationships.

Later, as a teenager, I became friends with another girl whose parents adopted her at birth. Like my childhood friend, she was a part of a solid, loving family. I witnessed the close relationship they shared and was very intrigued by the topic of adoption. I even decided to write an article in the high school newspaper on the subject. I will always remember my friend's response when I asked her what it felt like to be adopted. She smiled proudly and replied, "I feel *natural*." She felt like she belonged with them. They loved her and she loved them, just as they would have if they were biologically related. Once again, I witnessed the beauty of adoption.

Seeing happy, loving families was not my only experience with adoption as a young girl. I also got to see the other side of the coin. I became friends with a teenage birth mom. This girl was new to our school, and we started sitting together on the bus one day. I remember she was very nice, but there was a deep sadness in her eyes. At just sixteen years old, she appeared much older and more mature than most girls our age. I just knew right away that she had been through something big in her young life. I wanted to reach out to her and help, but at first I had no idea what I could do for her. How could I help when I didn't even know what was wrong? She must have sensed my empathy and knew that she could trust me because one day, she opened up and shared her story.

While at her previous school, she had gotten pregnant and given birth. Because she was so young, there was no way she could raise a baby on her own. Her mother encouraged her to place her infant boy for adoption. Although it was the most difficult thing she had ever done, she believed she had no other choice. She wanted her baby to have a good life.

For months, my friend would talk to me about how she was feeling. I offered a shoulder for her to cry on and a sympathetic ear. I listened to her as she described her sorrow and pain. A part of me could feel her emotions and her suffering. I felt sad for this girl and what she was dealing with. She loved this little boy with all her heart and missed him like crazy. She wondered how he was doing and if he was safe, happy, and healthy. She longed to see him and hold him. There was this deep, persistent ache in her heart that wouldn't go away. Not a day went by when she didn't think of him. She felt like she had been torn apart from someone who was very much a part of her. She felt alone and empty inside. She was grieving the biggest loss of her young life.

I believe all three of these girls were put into

my life for a reason. I was meant to see what it was like to be a part of an adoptive family and to witness what a birth parent goes through when she places her child for adoption. Having these experiences helped me understand adoption better and prepare me for the future adoption of my own child. I was able to get an in-depth look at the bigger picture. I am so incredibly grateful to these friends for showing me the many emotions involved in adoption and giving me insight that I couldn't have otherwise gained.

So when I say to follow your instincts and choose the path that feels right for you, this is what I mean. For me, adoption was the only choice. It was the culmination of my life experiences. My heart led me to adoption and had been guiding me there for years.

Of course, not everyone is going to have such a profound and clear-cut experience. I don't expect that all couples who choose adoption can tell you that they have had so many indicators that influenced their decision. But what we do all have is a sense of intuition that helps guide us. As you choose your next step, be sure to stop and listen to what your inner voice is telling you. Don't just rely on intellect to decide what to do. Instead, look deep inside yourself and go by what you *feel*. Which path feels right? Once you've identified that, you'll know what to do next.

After suffering two miscarriages, the natural next step for us was to explore adoption as a potential way to create our family. We were ready to consider the possibilities!

"Not flesh of my flesh, nor bone of my bone,
yet still miraculously my own
Never forget for a single minute,
you didn't grow under my heart, but in it."
—*Fleur Conkling Heyliger*

CHAPTER 9: CONSIDERING ADOPTION

Choosing to adopt is definitely not a decision to take lightly. Then again, neither is the decision to become a parent by any method. You need to be certain you're ready and able to take on such a big responsibility. It's also important to understand what you may or may not experience as a result of adopting a child. You may have some reservations or be reluctant to consider adoption because you know you will not be biologically related to your child. You may be feeling sad or disappointed that you will not carry on your own genes or family heritage. Some couples question: "Will I love my baby?" or "What if he or she is different from me?" You may wonder if it will be difficult to raise a child who does not share similar traits or characteristics as you. You may even have difficulty letting go of the desire to have a growing baby inside of you and give birth.

Before we adopted, we discussed all of these potential concerns. Losing two babies and coming to the realization that I was never going to give birth to my child was a tremendous disappointment. There was a very strong and persistent maternal instinct inside of me. I wanted to create a baby. I wanted to feel that child growing inside of me. I longed to experience the miracle of childbirth and safely bring a baby into the world. And I had envisioned our child resembling my husband and me. I had expected that he or she would share similar interests and passions, and inherit some of our talents. So, along with suffering two miscarriages, I had to come to terms with another loss: the loss of the baby I had imagined and planned for. I had to learn to accept that this person I had created in my mind would never exist. My dream—the one I had planned for since childhood—was over.

That certainly didn't mean I wanted to just give up on my dream altogether. I knew I needed to find another way to make it happen. My instinct to become a mother was just too strong to toss aside.

After grieving our losses and shedding many tears, Paul and I were ready to reevaluate our lives and priorities. I knew I definitely did not want to attempt another pregnancy. Quite frankly, the treatment plan I would need to follow scared me, and I just couldn't bear any more medical drama or devastating losses.

The way I saw it, we had two options: surrogacy or adoption. If we hired a surrogate, I would need to undergo a medical procedure to remove eggs from my ovaries, which entailed being under anesthesia and dealing with more doctors. In addition, there was a chance our child could inherit my blood clotting disorder and have the same problem having a baby that I had. No thanks. I had enough of hospitals and doctors and didn't want anyone messing with my body again. I also didn't want my child to one day experience the same heartbreak I had. Surrogacy just didn't feel like the right choice for us. So we moved on to discussing adoption.

We knew that with adoption, our dreams of parenthood could finally be realized. We could even bring home an infant if we chose the domestic program. However, the adoption process is often unpredictable, so we would need to be flexible and willing to accept the uncertainty. Also, our child would not be biologically related to us. He or she may look totally different and have a personality in stark contrast to our own. Could we accept this? Would we love this child as our own? Or would we feel like we were raising a stranger or just babysitting someone else's kid?

Paul and I did a lot of soul-searching and

talked at length about the pros and cons of adoption. We discussed what parenthood meant to us and what we hoped to achieve. We concluded that what we wanted most was to be parents. We wanted to love, teach, nurture, protect, and guide a child. We agreed that it was not necessary to carry on our own genes. It didn't matter to either one of us if our child had different interests and mannerisms. We didn't need him or her to look just like us. After considering all of the factors, we decided that adoption seemed like the best way for us to build our family.

Coming to that conclusion didn't eliminate all of our concerns. Like most potential adoptive parents, we still wondered what this type of parenting would be like. Would raising an adopted child somehow seem inferior? Would we still feel like we were missing out on something? At the time, we didn't know the answers to these questions. Although I had no doubt we would love our child, I didn't know if the experience would equal that of being a biological parent.

You may have these same questions and concerns about adopting. As someone who has already been through it, I know for certain that genetics is far less important than most people think. Will you love your child? Absolutely.

I can tell you from personal experience that I could not imagine loving my daughter any more if she had been born to me. Our bond is strong, and our love is deep. There is no doubt that I am her mother, and she is my child.

Jason Bradley-Krauss and his family are also proof of the incredible love and connection adoptive parents have with their kids. Jason and his partner Chris are proud fathers of two children from Guatemala.

"My children are my life," says Jason. "I am a part of them, and they are a part of me. Their tears are my tears. Their joy, my joy. My life has a new purpose—larger than caring for myself. With children, you see your life in the context of generations."

It's clear that there is a lot of love in adoptive families, but you may still wonder, "Will adopting a child feel different in some way?"

My family may not have been created in the traditional way, but it is very much like any other family. In fact, I must admit that most of the time I don't even remember that my daughter was adopted—and neither does the rest of my family. It feels like she belongs with us. She is one of us. We certainly don't need biology to tell us that. We feel it every day. We feel it when she smiles or gives us a hug. We feel it when we are on vacation at our summer home up north, or at Cedar Point, Traverse City, or Disney World. We feel it when we help her with her homework or put a Band-Aid on her scraped knee. We feel it when we read her a story and tuck her into bed at night. Our experiences, our joys, our worries, and our fears are the same as every parent out there.

Other people don't view us any differently either and often have no idea that we are not biologically related. They remark that our daughter must have gotten her height from her father, but it never occurs to them that her height didn't come from either of us. When we tell people our daughter is adopted, they are often surprised. And they are always very accepting of our family situation and think the fact that we adopted our child is wonderful. Some even view it as a selfless act of kindness or a way of making the world a better place by caring for a child in need. They think it is admirable to raise a baby who was conceived and born to someone else. Although I've always wanted to help others and make a difference in the world, I don't feel like a saint or someone who is doing a kind deed. I just feel like a regular mom.

It's true not sharing genes makes our children different than us, but that certainly has no bearing on the love you feel or the success of your family. It also doesn't mean that you will have nothing in common with your kids. You'll find your kids complement you with a refreshing mix of unique traits and comforting similarities. You may even find some traits or talents in your child that you wish you had or that you can learn something from.

My daughter has blond hair and blue eyes. Because I have brown hair and brown eyes, I had always wished for blond hair and blue eyes as a child. I am short, and my daughter very tall. Ironically, when I look at her, I see a reflection of the person I wanted to be as a child. As far as her personality, she is independent, outgoing, silly, impulsive, athletic, feisty, and often fearless—all things I was not growing up. She has a natural music ability and can play the piano by ear, something I find very difficult to do. I find these differences interesting and am often glad my daughter is not just like me.

Despite our differences, my daughter and I also share some similarities. She is compassionate, empathic, and cares deeply about others. She loves to dance and enjoys the outdoors. She is intelligent, creative, and imaginative. She enjoys reading and excels at writing and math. Some of this may be learned; some may be genetic. But the point is: it really doesn't matter. Our family works.

Sure, there are challenges. Our daughter is very high-strung, excitable, and easily distracted. Sometimes she has trouble focusing, listening, or sitting still. Because of her busy mind and active personality, she sometimes has difficulty sleeping and wakes up during the night. When she does, she often spends hours talking, thinking, and asking questions, just like she would in the middle of the day. There are nights when I'm exhausted and wish she would just go to sleep. But these are the types of challenges *all* parents face. They have nothing to do with the fact that she is adopted. The love I feel for my daughter is strong and real and deep. We are connected through this love. I truly believe she was destined to be a part of our family.

So if you question whether or not you can raise a child not born to you, the answer is: yes, you can! Many adoptive mothers will tell you, "My child may not have grown in my belly, but she grew in my heart." That statement is so true and will give you an idea of the joy that adoption brings. Genetics may make us similar to our family members, but love is what connects us. Remember that as you embark on your own amazing journey to find the family you were meant to have.

"One's destination is never a place,
but rather a new way of looking at things."
—Henry Miller

CHAPTER 10: BEGINNING THE ADOPTION PROCESS

Beginning your own adoption journey is a very exciting time in your life. Disappointment and sadness are replaced with hope for the future, as you anticipate finally becoming a parent. Your journey to adopt will be unique to you, and you will learn so much along the way—both about the process itself and about the type of family you would like to create.

You'll likely do a lot of thinking and may consider various options. There are so many choices available to you, such as domestic newborn adoption; international adoption of a baby, toddler, or school-age child; or foster care adoption of a child or sibling group of all ages. For some, the desire to have a newborn will draw them to domestic adoption. This route offers the chance to bond with your child from the beginning. You'll also likely have the opportunity to meet with your baby's birth parents and maintain some ongoing contact, if all parties agree. The downside is that you will have to wait for a potential birth parent to actually choose you, so the time frame is unpredictable.

If you choose domestic newborn adoption, it's important to try to put yourself in a potential birth parent's shoes and imagine what it might feel like to be them. Be empathic and a good listener. And never put any pressure or expectations on potential birth parents. Let them know you will answer any questions they have and give them time and space to make the decision that is right for both them and their unborn child.

Some of you may opt for international adoption, which eliminates the need to be selected by a birth parent and usually offers the opportunity to travel. International adoption is typically more expensive than domestic adoption. You will have a wonderful chance to learn about your child's birth country and customs, but will typically not meet the birth parents or receive any family health history. You won't need to be selected by a potential birth mom and will instead receive a referral for a child. Many children adopted internationally are living in orphanages or foster homes. Infants are available, but depending on the country you choose, their ages will range from six months to one year old. Most of the time, you cannot choose the gender of your child, unless you already have a child of the opposite gender.

Another option is to adopt an older child or sibling group waiting in the foster care system. This is by far the least expensive choice. Many times you can adopt a child from foster care for just the cost of your home study, which is typically around $2,000–3,000. There is a great need for parents to adopt older children or sibling groups. Most of these kids have been removed from their homes due to abuse and/or neglect and really need a family to love and take care of them. The downside is the many challenges that come with parenting a troubled child. Because of their traumatic pasts, these kids often have learning disabilities or emotional problems that will require a lot of time and patience to address. Some common issues affecting abused or neglected children are: attachment disorders, oppositional defiant disorder (ODD), fetal alcohol syndrome (FAS), drug exposure, sexual abuse, domestic violence, attention deficit disorder (ADD), attention deficit hyperactivity disorder (ADHD), depression, anxiety, bipolar disorder, and various mental illnesses. But despite these challenges, many happy, loving, successful families are formed this way.

The path you choose to pursue will depend on many factors, including your personal preferences, time constraints, your age, and even the amount of money you have. Sometimes you will change paths after learning more about what the various types of adoption entail. You'll discover—through the situations you encounter and the people you meet—exactly what you are willing and able to handle in your life. This is all part of the fascinating, exciting world of adoption.

After the losses and disappointments my husband and I experienced in the past, adoption gave us an amazing sense of hope. We could still have the family we dreamed of! Somewhere out there was a special child for us to love and care for. It was an exhilarating time in our lives. We couldn't wait to get started.

In July 2003, I began researching adoption agencies with the intent to adopt a baby or toddler domestically. I visited agency websites and requested information by mail from the ones that looked promising. Paul and I then narrowed down our list to two agencies and made plans to meet with them.

Most agencies have group gatherings for prospective adoptive parents to learn more about their organization and the programs available. If the agency doesn't offer this service, you can request a one-on-one meeting with an adoption professional.

You can also hire an adoption attorney instead of, or in addition to, hiring an agency. The attorney will specialize in managing the adoption process for both adoptive families and birth parents. An attorney is not necessary to complete an adoption, as long as you are working with a licensed adoption agency and meet the state requirements.

Before you hire any adoption professional, it is important to have your questions answered, so you know what to expect during the process and can determine if the agency or attorney is the right fit for you. We came up with a list of questions to ask and brought them with us when meeting with adoption professionals. (You'll find the list of questions on pages 107–108.)

We attended our first informational meeting in August 2003. The agency was a large, successful local organization. About twenty to thirty couples gathered in a conference room for a presentation. At the meeting, a few representatives spoke about the agency, the adoption process, and the various programs available. We even heard personal stories from couples who had successfully adopted through them. It was an encouraging and enlightening experience.

Despite an impressive presentation, our instincts told us that this was not the right agency for us. For one, this large agency seemed much like a "business" rather than a nonprofit organization designed to help people. During the meeting, a representative talked about money and placed a strong emphasis on couples covering birth parent expenses. She stated that they require potential adoptive couples to set up an escrow account containing several thousand dollars for this purpose. Although we had no problem helping a birth mother out financially if she truly needed it, we didn't feel that should automatically be expected in every case. We felt uncomfortable with this agency's approach, since the primary focus should be on finding a good, loving home for a child, not promising expectant mothers large sums of money. So we moved on.

We met with the director of another adoption agency in September 2003. This agency was much smaller, and we felt comfortable right away. The director was compassionate, honest, and knowledgeable. She told us that they don't place an emphasis on birth parent expenses because they believe the focus needs to be on finding a good home for a child. We were so happy to hear this!

The director also patiently and thoroughly addressed our concerns and answered our questions. She even recommended books we could read for further information. And she was very honest about what to expect. When we asked how long the wait to adopt domestically was, she said that she couldn't give us a set time frame because there isn't a "waiting list." Potential birth parents choose adoptive parents based on their profiles. She also added that one family adopted in as little as six months, but another had been waiting four years and still didn't have a child yet. My heart sank when I heard that. My wait to become a mother had already seemed like an eternity. I just couldn't imagine waiting four more years! Sensing my disappointment, the director assured me the agency would do whatever they could to support us during the process, but to expect a long wait. She also encouraged us to network and spread the word we were planning to adopt to help increase our chances of finding a child sooner.

During our conversation, we got the impression the staff genuinely cares about all parties involved in the adoption and does their best to help everyone. I remember sitting across from the director just knowing that this was the beginning of our journey. It just felt right.

We left the agency excited and hopeful and soon after completed our preliminary application. The initial application asks for basic information, such as your ages, places of employment, income, and reasons for wanting to adopt. We also needed to submit a small application fee. Our road to parenthood had begun!

If you decide to proceed with your own adoption, here are some questions you can ask that will help you select an agency.

Questions to Ask Adoption Professionals

1) How long have you been in business?
2) What programs do you offer?
3) Are there any age requirements for your programs?
4) Is it possible to switch programs during the process?
5) Are you required to travel for an international adoption?
6) What are the approximate costs to adopt?

7) Are we required to pay for birth parent expenses?

8) About how many placements do you make per year?

9) How many families do you have waiting to adopt?

10) Approximately how long can I expect to wait before successfully adopting?

11) Once I've completed my application, how soon will I be contacted to begin the home study?

12) How long does a home study typically take?

13) Do you offer the option of having an online profile?

14) What services do you provide after the adoption?

Once you've met with some adoption professionals, you will not only be more knowledgeable about the process, but you will also be ready to make a decision about which agency or attorney you would like to work with.

I urge you to trust your instincts and pick the professional that *feels* like the best fit for your family and your circumstances. In our case, we chose the one we felt most comfortable with after researching several agencies. We agreed with their philosophy on adoption and liked that they were a smaller, more personal agency.

After you've selected an agency and your preliminary application is approved, the next step is completing the detailed formal application, which is just the beginning of the mounds of paperwork required for an adoption. I must say that the paperwork is very tedious and time-consuming. I thought buying a house had a lot of documents! Clearly, adoption has home ownership beat! I admit that sometimes I felt like we would never get through it all. But I did my best to complete everything as quickly as possible because I knew the sooner we got through it, the closer we would be to adopting our child.

To apply to adopt, we gathered several personal documents, including our driver's licenses, marriage license, financial statements, and income tax returns. We were required to have credit and background checks, references from employers and friends, and physicals from our family doctor. We also completed autobiographies on our lives, family history, upbringing, and philosophy on parenting. (For more information on the requirements to adopt, see pages 184–186.)

If you pursue a domestic adoption, your agency may also want you to become licensed as a foster family. We did this, and I can assure you it is not as complicated as it sounds. We simply completed a few hours of training and filled out some paperwork to receive our foster license. My husband and I attended a training seminar in Lansing, Michigan, through the Michigan Adoption Resource Exchange (MARE). The seminar was called Parents As

Tender Healers (PATH) and discussed such topics as: understanding hurt children, the impact of loss on children, surviving crisis, and helping a child become a part of your family. We completed several exercises and participated in group discussions that allowed us the opportunity to brainstorm ways to solve problems and help children. The training gave us a better understanding of the way children behave and why, which is certainly a plus for anyone without parenting experience.

Adopting may sound like a lot of work, but it actually goes pretty smoothly. Please don't let the paperwork and adoption agency requirements discourage you. They really aren't a big deal, and I actually found some of it to be quite fun. I enjoyed writing my autobiography and learning all about the adoption process. I also enjoyed the training seminar and the valuable insight it provided. And I was very grateful for the incredible support and encouragement we received. Keep in mind that the adoption agency staff and social workers are there every step of the way to answer questions and help guide you through the process. Everyone at our agency was very patient and helpful. They care about all parties involved—the birth parents, adoptive parents, and most importantly, the child. They will do whatever they can to make sure that everyone is comfortable with the situation and that there is a good fit between the birth parents and the adoptive parents.

After the formal application process was

complete, we were contacted by a licensed social worker to begin our home study. This typically includes four to six visits in your home. We began our home study in November 2003.

I remember all the feelings that went along with this next crucial step in our journey to become parents. On one hand, we were excited, hopeful and eager to proceed with our home study. We felt like we were on our way to becoming parents! On the other hand, we felt a bit apprehensive to meet with a social worker. We wondered if during the home study our lives, personalities, and history would be scrutinized. I was nervous about making a good impression and proving that we would be wonderful parents. Even though I knew this in my heart, I had to convince someone else. I felt like this was some sort of a test, and I didn't want to fail!

My fears were quickly alleviated at our first meeting with the social worker. As intimidating as a home study sounds, it turned out to be quite different than what I expected. Our social worker was friendly and knowledgeable. She wasn't there to judge us or test us; she was there to educate us. She was there to help guide us through the process and ensure that we were equipped with the necessary knowledge and skills to become adoptive parents.

During her visits to our home, our social worker discussed the adoption process with us. She helped us complete the necessary paperwork and answered our questions. She also inspected our home and made sure it was in compliance with the laws of our state. This does not mean you have to have a large or spotless home. It simply means that your house needs to be safe and adequate for a child to comfortably live in. For example, we were required to have smoke detectors on every floor, as well as a carbon monoxide detector. We also developed a fire safety plan, which detailed what we would do in the event of a fire. In addition, our social worker made sure there was adequate sleeping space to accommodate a child. She also wrote a report with a description of our life circumstances and home environment.

After a couple of meetings, we were quite pleased with how smoothly our home study was going. I laughed at how I had once been nervous and worried about it. But just because our adoption process was proceeding nicely, it didn't mean our lives were free from challenges. Partway through our home study, Paul's father became very ill. He had been diagnosed with leukemia twelve years earlier and had been through periods of chemotherapy and remission. Now, he also had lymphoma. He went through radiation to shrink a tumor in his neck, with some success. However, he also had breathing problems and a tumor in his lung. We sadly watched him fight for his life as he bravely battled one obstacle after another. He kept hanging on and trying to get better. His will to live was strong.

We visited him in the hospital several times and told him all about our efforts to adopt a child. Each time we would come, he was always very interested in hearing more. Although he was frail, weak, and very sick, there was a noticeable change in him whenever we would talk about our adoption. He face would light up, and he would smile. He was a gentle, quiet man, and his love for children and family was evident. Those were the things that kept him going.

Unfortunately, despite his fighting spirit and the best efforts of his doctors, we watched his condition deteriorate. He lost partial hearing in his ear due to the radiation. He also suffered damage to his esophagus and needed a feeding tube. His cancer affected his lungs, which resulted in a tracheotomy to help him breathe and pulmonary surgery. But his cancer was just too advanced. He lost a lot of blood, almost died during the surgery, and was temporarily put on a respirator. There was nothing more the doctors could do.

As Paul and I were working hard to start our own family, his dad was slipping away day by day. The family was in turmoil. Dealing with Paul's dad's illness and watching him suffer was heartbreaking and extremely difficult. In addition to being immersed in the adoption process, we were struggling to cope with a major family crisis. It was a very busy, stressful, and emotional time in our lives—filled with many tears, long talks, prayers, and lots of consoling hugs.

I remember dividing my time and energy between our adoption efforts and supporting my husband and his family. Surprisingly, I turned out to be the strong one through all of this. I was very helpful and supportive to my mother-in-law. I was there for my husband and his family. I did whatever I could to help them and comfort them through a very difficult time.

Sadly, in the middle of our home study, Paul's dad passed away. The whole family gathered at the hospital during his final hours. He tried several times to talk but was unable to. I believe he just wanted to let everyone know how much he cared about them and say his final good-byes. He was able to convey to my husband that he loved him before he died.

I remember watching Paul's dad take his last breath. It was truly the hardest thing I have ever witnessed. Seeing someone die changes you. You are filled with overwhelming sorrow. You feel powerless over life's circumstances. It is a real shock to see someone once so full of life just lying there still and lifeless. You are reminded of how short life really is. It is at that point that you fully realize the magnitude of life and death. And you remember that love and family are at the center of your existence. Nothing else matters but the connections we have in this life. Every person you have ever loved has shaped you into the person you are today. Without them, your life would be empty and meaningless.

Thinking about the importance of family and love made us want to start our own family even more. We continued along our adoption journey with the next step in the process: writing a letter to potential birth parents. In my opinion, your letter is one of the most important tools in the adoption process. You want to make sure you take your time and really think about what you want to say and what you want potential birth parents to know about you and your family.

Our letter contained photos of us and gave information about our lives to help pregnant women decide if we were the right family to raise their child. It is your chance to introduce yourselves to a potential birth mom and provide some insight into who you are and what type of parents you will be. Often, potential birth moms will choose adoptive parents who have similar interests and backgrounds as them. Sometimes, they will select a couple who looks like them. Or they may choose a family based on the feeling they get from reading your profile. It is important to be honest and speak from your heart, so birth parents will really get a sense of who you are. This increases the chances that the adoption will be successful.

To give you an idea of what a "Dear Birth Parent" letter is like, take a look at our letter on pages 116–117.

We're Looking for a Special Child to Love

Dear Birth Mother,

We know you are faced with a difficult decision and hope that we can help ease the anxiety you must be feeling.

We have always wanted to be parents and believe that adoption is the best way to build our family. After losing two children to miscarriage, we learned that Deanna has a condition that causes recurrent pregnancy loss. We decided not to pursue another pregnancy due to the risks involved.

Although we have not yet had the opportunity to raise a child, we feel that we are parents in our hearts. We've envisioned our family many times and have dreamed of sharing the beauty of the world with a child—whether we're visiting the zoo, feeding the ducks in our backyard, or helping a child learn and explore.

We have a lot of love to give and believe that every child deserves the best possible chance at life. In addition to a good, loving home, we will give your child an abundance of nurturing, support, and guidance.

Both of us are creative and enjoy teaching and helping others. While in college, Deanna worked as a writing tutor for underprivileged freshmen, and Paul helped college students grasp difficult formulas and concepts as a math tutor. Today, Paul is a senior project engineer, and Deanna works part-time from home as a business writer. She plans to be a stay-at-home mom.

We are very excited about becoming parents. We come from loving and supportive families, who are eagerly awaiting the arrival of a new family member. In addition, we live in a nice family neighborhood with a large backyard, swing set, and excellent schools. What matters most, however, is our compassion and strong desire to make a positive difference in a child's life. We look forward to the day when we can finally do that as parents.

We appreciate you taking the time to learn more about us and wish you all the best as you make a very important decision.

Sincerely,
Paul & Deanna

Our letter also included a side bar with bullet points that highlighted our hobbies and interests. In addition, we listed our adoption agency's phone number, so potential birth parents would have it handy if they had additional questions about us or the adoption process. I designed our letter using Microsoft Publisher and had it printed in color at a copy shop. Some agencies offer the option of posting your birth parent letter and profile online. I highly recommend doing this. It makes your information readily accessible day or night and increases your chances of being seen and chosen by a potential birth parent.

Once your letter is finished and your home study is complete, you begin the waiting. This is by far the hardest part of the adoption process. When our home study was finished in January 2004, we were very excited and felt like we were well on our way to finally becoming parents.

If adoption sounds intriguing, I can assure you, it is. However, it's important to remember that even though you are thrilled to be starting the adoption process, it is not a quick and easy way to build a family. I'm sure you've heard the line "We'll just adopt!" in movies, in books, and on television. When a couple has trouble conceiving or can't have a baby the traditional way, adoption is seen as an easy solution. Adoption is often portrayed as glamorous and simple. This is especially true in Hollywood, where we hear stories all the time about movie stars adopting children. It all seems effortless. In reality, this is far from the truth.

Adoption is anything but easy. It is a very complex, sometimes expensive, and time-consuming process. I've heard it described as "an emotional roller coaster," "a pregnancy without a due date," and "not for the faint of heart."

As someone who was in the adoption process for more than two years, I've learned that all of these statements are true. Trying to adopt can indeed be an overwhelming, frustrating, and very emotional time in your life. I'm not saying this to discourage you. I just want to be honest about what we experienced and prepare you for what lies ahead. Don't expect adoption to be fast or easy. Prepare to wait. Expect delays. If you choose domestic newborn adoption, know that even when a potential birth mom expresses an interest in you or actually chooses you to parent her baby, that it still may not happen.

This is true no matter what type of adoption you choose to pursue—domestic, international, or foster care. There are always unexpected happenings that may even steer you in a different direction than you started.

When Jason Bradley-Krauss and his partner Chris decided to pursue international adoption in 2002, they were excited and couldn't wait to become fathers. They originally chose to adopt from Ukraine and happily embarked on their adoption journey. After nine months of planning, preparing, and completing all the required paperwork, they were in the final phase of the process—waiting for a referral for their child. It was at this point, they learned the shocking truth. It turns out the success of adopting from that country involved a customary gesture of gift giving. The larger and more expensive the gift, the more likely you were to bring home a healthy baby. Jason says some couples who had been through the process recommended bringing $10,000 in cash just to get in and out of the country safely. Jason and Chris were horrified by this and just couldn't be a part of such a questionable practice. Sadly, they backed out of the program.

"The day we decided not to go through with our adoption was very painful," says Jason. "I sobbed as I felt my dreams of fatherhood slip away. I grieved for the child I had imagined in my mind—I felt like I was failing him or her."

Jason and Chris discussed other options and ended up contacting another agency they had spoken with before. They then chose to pursue an adoption from Guatemala.

The point is: there are so many unknowns when adopting. It's important to be aware of the potential obstacles you could face and to expect the unexpected. It's not always smooth sailing, and everyone's journey has a unique set of challenges.

On the positive side, the rewards of adopting are phenomenal—and definitely worth the risk! At the end of the process, you will have the most miraculous gift you could ever ask for: your child, the child that was meant to be a part of your family. And that is worth anything the adoption process might entail.

After our home study was complete, we were eager to more forward. We were ready for the roller coaster ride of ups and downs that would one day lead us to our child. At the time, we had no idea what a ride it would be or how long the wait would feel.

"Patience and perseverance have a magical effect
before which difficulties disappear
and obstacles vanish."
—John Quincy Adams

CHAPTER 11: RIDING THE ADOPTION ROLLER COASTER

Once you've finished your home study, it's time to get ready for quite an interesting ride. You'll soon discover that adoption is very much like a roller coaster, with many ups and downs. There really is no other way I can think of to describe it.

Consider this: with both adoption and roller coasters, you wait eagerly in anticipation to experience it. Once on the roller coaster, you are filled with many conflicting emotions—fear, excitement, exhilaration, and uncertainty. It is part fun and part scary at the same time. The hills can sometimes seem intimidating and overwhelming.

The ride can be bumpy. And, of course, there are the ups and downs! All of these things accurately describe adoption.

Throughout the process, we were faced with many ups and downs. This is normal and all part of the journey. Some days you will feel hopeful that you'll soon become parents. Other days you'll feel like it will never happen. My mood fluctuated from being excited and looking forward to having a child to being sad, frustrated, and depressed when nothing happened.

Sometimes, people adopt quickly—but that is not the norm. It is typically a long wait, often two years or more for a domestic Caucasian newborn. The wait to adopt internationally can also be quite long, with most parents waiting at least one year and some as long as three years to bring home their child. Just know going into the process that you will need to be patient and stay positive.

"Have faith that things will work out the way they're meant to be," suggests Christina Molby, who spent more than two years in the adoption process before being matched with her son's birth parents. "Even though you might not agree or understand it now, there's a bigger plan at work."

Also remember that you don't have to just sit and wait for your adoption agency to call you with a potential situation. There is so much you can do while you are waiting to not only pass the time, but also expand your knowledge and increase your chances of successfully adopting.

Because I am not the type of person to sit

around and wait, I focused much of my time and energy on finding a child. I did everything in my power to spread the word that we were interested in adopting and also provide ways for potential birth parents to find us. First, I wrote a letter to friends and family letting them know of our desire to adopt a child and asking them to keep us in mind if they heard of any potential situations. Next, I set up a dedicated e-mail address and got a toll-free number that would ring at our home for potential birth parents to contact us anytime. Then I created business cards to place on bulletin boards, leave in public places, and give to friends and family. We purchased business card paper at an office supply store and printed our cards on our home printer.

Your business cards should include your first names, e-mail address, phone number, and adoption agency name and number, as well as a heading that will quickly catch someone's attention. Something like: "Pregnant? Considering Adoption?" or "We Want to Adopt." If someone you know hears of a woman considering adoption, you can simply give him or her a card to pass along. In addition, we placed an advertisement in the classified section of a local newspaper.

As I mentioned, my husband and I also attended a training seminar on adopting children through the foster care system. We had the opportunity to talk to professionals and learn about some of the issues and concerns that abused and neglected children often face. The social workers at the training class also offered parenting strategies for how best to handle problems that arise because of past trauma in these children's lives. Although we chose not to adopt a waiting child, the seminar was very enlightening and made us more empathic and aware of the many children in need.

Another tool I used was the Internet. I discovered some wonderful websites where I could go to do research, ask questions, and get advice from others who were trying to adopt or had already successfully adopted. At the sites, I met people who were at all stages of the adoption process. The ones who had successfully adopted gave me hope and encouragement. The ones who had suffered losses or encountered obstacles offered sympathy. It was like being a part of a large interconnected circle, where everyone understood me and had the same questions, the same fears, and the same hopes.

I found the Internet to be one of the most useful and valuable resources throughout the adoption process. There is a wealth of information out there that can really help to not only educate you about adoption, but also provide support and even some tools to increase your chances of adopting sooner. For support and education, I highly recommend adoption.com. The site is huge and features articles, blogs, the latest news, photo listings, and more. You'll find resources for all stages of the adoption process, including how to get started, the various types of adoptions, current laws and issues, and parenting tips. In addition to helping educate those who are considering adopting, the site offers a wealth of information for birth parents, such as how to cope with an unplanned pregnancy and how to decide what to do. And adoptees will find articles on reunion, common issues, and stories from others in similar situations. Adoption.com is also home to an awesome discussion forum, forums.adoption.com. There you will find thousands of women just like you from all around the country. Some have miscarried. Some have dealt with infertility. Some are trying to adopt. And others have successfully adopted. It is a fantastic place to ask questions, vent your frustrations, and share your excitement. Many of the people there have been exactly where you are right now—and they know how you feel! They also know what worked for them and can offer helpful advice and suggestions. Along with support and education, you'll find several websites that feature children waiting in the foster care system and a few that have situations involving pregnant women. Some of the sites I visited were: adoptuskids.org, mare.org, adoptionsituations.com, and adoptex.org.

There are even some websites that allow you to post your adoption profile online for a fee. We signed up with parentprofiles.com and created an online profile that was accessible to potential birth parents from across the country. This turned out to be one of the most effective tools we found for attracting prospective birth parents. We received several leads from our profile, some by phone and others by e-mail. A couple of the women actually contacted our agency, and one even met us at a restaurant. If you decide to create a profile online, just keep in mind that there may be many women who contact you who are very early in the decision-making process and may ultimately decide to parent their children. You need to be patient and prepared for some disappointments along the way. But I believe the more resources you use, the better your chances for adopting successfully and more quickly, so it's definitely worth a try!

As you can see, adoption became like a full-time job for me. I spent several hours each day reading, researching, networking, and searching for waiting children in the foster care system. I also created a blog called "Our Journey to Parenthood," where I wrote about our experiences throughout the adoption process. This became a great outlet for my thoughts and feelings. I poured my heart and soul into my quest to become a mom. I was driven. I was passionate. I wanted to become a mom more than anything and was determined to make it happen.

I truly believe that if you want something badly enough, you can find a way to bring your dreams to fruition. Just know that you are in this to the end. Believe that you will become a parent one day and do all you can to stay positive and make it happen.

Another bit of advice I have that will help you on your journey is to be open and understanding to the many different situations you will encounter and the many different people you will meet. Adoption is a very complex subject, filled with much emotion for everyone involved. You may encounter a distraught birth mom who is struggling with financial difficulties, drug addiction, or other hardships. You may meet a child who has never had a family and has lived in an orphanage. Or you may encounter an angry, emotionally fragile, or wounded child who has suffered abuse.

Try to be empathic to those you encounter and put yourself in their shoes. Then assess whether or not you can integrate these people and their experiences into your own life and family. Don't rule anything out until you've had plenty of time to explore your options. As I've said, you will come to know what is right for you based on how you feel.

"Don't go into the process close-minded. Be open to various situations," recommends adoptive parent Christina Molby. "You could be surprised. Adoption has changed my life tremendously and led me down a different path than I would have ever expected."

"Children are our most precious natural resource."
—Herbert Hoover

CHAPTER 12: CHILDREN IN NEED

At one point in our adoption journey, we had seriously considered adopting an older child or sibling group from foster care. I especially felt compelled to help these poor hurt children who were victims of unfortunate circumstances. My heart ached when I read about the suffering they endured, and I kept thinking that if someone would just love, support, and protect them, that they could heal and live a normal happy childhood. I still do believe this is possible, but I learned the issues these children face and the severity of their problems can often make functioning normally a real challenge.

I'll never forget two sibling groups we were being considered for. They were both out of state, one in Texas and the other in Colorado. Their pictures portrayed adorable, lovable children who looked happy and well-adjusted. However, behind the innocent eyes and bright smiles were some of the most disturbing and horrifying circumstances I had ever encountered.

After we submitted our home study to the social services offices in the children's home states, we received their social history reports to review. These reports contain details about the kids' backgrounds, including information on their birth families, medical problems, and any issues they are experiencing. The first group of siblings we fell in love with were two sisters, ages four and six. One girl was very creative and loved to draw and color. The other enjoyed playing outside on the monkey bars. They were beautiful, lovable, sweet children. But they were unfortunate victims of circumstances.

These girls had come from a past of domestic violence, involving knives and guns. Their birth father was in jail, and their birth mother was labeled as being "borderline intellectual functioning" and had difficulty caring for the kids in the appropriate way. She was unable to control the girls and often screamed or hit them to try to get them to obey. Although the younger girl was preschool age, she was still in diapers and had severe diaper rash from not being changed very often. The older daughter was sexually abused by an adult relative. The report mentioned that the younger child was especially violent. She threatened her foster mother with a knife and stabbed her older sister, sending her to the emergency room. She also hit her baby brother very hard and injured him. They had been in and out of foster homes because most families couldn't seem to handle them and ended up fearing for their own safety. But despite their problems, these girls were still just helpless, young children. They needed a family to love them, support them, and help them get on the right path.

I remember that desperate longing in my heart to help these children. I sat on our couch crying for them one day. They really needed someone. It hurt inside just thinking of all they had been through. As I wondered whether or not we could take on such a difficult and challenging situation, my husband asked me a very important question: "Do you want to help them or do you want to be their mom?"

I pondered that question for a few minutes and quickly realized that I was not equipped to deal with such severe problems. I had absolutely no experience as a mom, let alone the mother of abused and violent children. As much as I wanted to reach out and help these poor kids in need, I did not really want to be their mom. I just wanted to *save* them. I had no desire to invite violence and instability into my home. And I certainly didn't want to try to be their mom, only to find out that I couldn't handle it. That wouldn't be fair to them. They had experienced enough heartbreak and disruptions in their young lives. They needed a secure, stable family life with parents who could stand by them forever no matter what. Although I have a lot of love in my heart and adore kids, I am often sensitive and emotional. I have been blessed with the gift of empathy, which allows me to feel great compassion for others, but at the same time, I often take on others' pain and problems and feel them as if they were my own. As much as I wanted to help these girls, I was not the tough, firm, rock-solid parent they needed. I hoped and prayed that these girls would find the right family, but I knew deep inside that family was not us.

Then came the next sibling group, a six-year-old girl and a four-year-old boy. These children also had serious issues. Both suffered from severe developmental delays and emotional problems. When they were first found, they had been living in a portable trailer in the woods. Neither child knew how to use eating utensils and exhibited animalistic behaviors. They didn't speak much and would grunt or growl as a way to communicate. The boy had an abnormally shaped head and a medical problem with his brain. There was the possibility that he may need surgery one day. The girl was sexually abused and was very flirtatious toward her foster father. According to the social history report, she would compete with her foster mom for her foster dad's attention and affection and was very seductive toward him. She had a lot of anger toward female authority figures and was very defiant toward her foster mother.

I remember thinking, "How is it possible for a six-year-old girl to be flirtatious and seductive? She shouldn't even know what that is, let alone how to act that way!" I just couldn't imagine having a daughter who was behaving that way toward my husband, her father. That was clearly a situation I was not prepared for or willing to accept and deal with. So after hearing yet another heartbreaking story of abuse and neglect, we decided that adopting from the foster care system was not for us and began to concentrate only on domestic newborn adoption.

Please keep in mind that not all children adopted from foster care have such severe problems. Some suffer from only mild issues and adjust well to their new homes. In addition, some parents have the time, energy, resources, and experience to really make a positive difference in these kids' lives. It all depends on your personality, your preferences, and your background. Trust your instincts. You will know if this type of adoption is right for you. For us, it wasn't.

You may need some extra patience, understanding, and resources when adopting a child with special needs. But there are many happy, successful families formed this way. For Darlene Zeutzius, a Wisconsin mom, foster care adoption turned out to be the right choice. She and her husband adopted a sibling group of three kids, ages eighteen months, four, and seven. Just three months after the adoption was finalized, they received a call asking if they would like to adopt their children's biological brother, age eight months. They happily accepted and are now the proud parents of five children, one biological and four adopted.

Darlene admits it hasn't always been easy.

"We have had a lot of therapy with one of our children. He tests our patience on a daily basis," says Darlene. "But in the end, he hugs me and tells me he loves me. If you ever ask him if he would rather live somewhere else, he will tell you that this is his home, and we are his family."

Darlene's daughter also had some difficulty adjusting following the adoption. She struggled with missing her birth mom in the beginning. Even though she never lived with her biological mother, it was hard for her to let go of the past. With time and effort, Darlene and her husband have helped her heal. Today, their daughter knows that it is okay to remember and miss her birth mom, and that her parents are there to help and support her. She also takes comfort in knowing that she can locate her birth mother when she is eighteen, with her parents' assistance, if she decides she wants to.

Despite some challenges, Darlene's family is happy and has a strong bond. The children are healthy and secure. They know they are loved and cherished. They know their parents will always be there to help nurture, protect, and guide them, as well as deal with any issues that arise. These are true signs of a successful family.

Darlene's advice for those interested in pursuing this type of adoption is to really know what you're looking for. Some questions she suggests asking yourself are: Do you want an infant? Do you want just one child? Do you care what race the child is? Do you want a relationship with the birth parents? Are you comfortable with not knowing a lot about your child's history? What are your expectations?

"You have to be strong in the sense of knowing there will be waves in your journey, and you are not in control of some of this," Darlene says. "You have to depend on social workers and agency workers and pray they are looking out for you."

Darlene recommends getting as much information as possible on your child and his or her birth family because once the adoption is complete, you will not receive any further details or have the opportunity to ask questions. In many cases, there are no longer any ties to the birth family.

She also says to remember to decide exactly what degree of special needs you are willing and able to accept. Some children will have mild issues and others will have very severe ones. Make sure you are educated on the various problems that exist and that you are equipped to successfully deal with them.

Even though we didn't believe we were up for the challenge of adopting special needs children from foster care, that doesn't mean that I regret pursuing it. I can honestly say that exploring foster care adoption was definitely a learning experience. I never imagined just how much these kids went through or how profoundly their pasts affected their feelings, behaviors, and even their academic performance. It helped open my eyes to the pain and suffering that some children endure.

When you long to be a mother, you envision a

happy family with a well-adjusted child. It's sad to think that this just isn't the case for some kids. As unfortunate as it is, some birth parents are just totally unprepared and ill-equipped to raise kids, but they do it anyway. They bring a child into the world and then struggle to provide a safe, stable home. They may be victims themselves of domestic violence, sexual abuse, or addictions. Some may suffer from financial difficulties or mental illnesses. Or they may simply be too young or immature to successfully parent a child.

The good news is that some women recognize that they just aren't able to parent a child. They know their own struggles and limitations. So rather than bring a child into a difficult or challenging life, they decide it's better to place their baby for adoption. I have great respect and admiration for these women. I also have a deep appreciation for them as well because without them, my dream of becoming a mom—and the dreams of thousands of others—may not have been possible. Their sacrifice is a precious gift to adoptive parents.

*"An invisible red thread connects those who
are destined to meet, regardless of time, place,
or circumstance. The thread may stretch
or tangle, but it will never break."*
—An ancient Chinese belief

CHAPTER 13: MEETING WITH POTENTIAL BIRTH PARENTS

When you are considering adoption, you often have many questions—not only about the process, but also about the people you'll meet and the situations you'll encounter. With every domestic adoption, you'll likely meet or talk to more than one potential birth mother. You may be wondering: What are these women like? What are their life circumstances? You may have an image in your mind of an unwed teenage girl. While this is certainly one example of a pregnant woman contemplating adoption, it is not the norm. The truth is that potential birth moms come from a variety of backgrounds and are all different ages. Some may be married or even divorced. Some have children already. Some have attended or are attending college. And although many are very young, there are also several who are in their twenties and thirties. My husband and I were in contact with many women who did not fit the traditional image.

During our adoption journey, we were matched with a potential birth mom Cindy* who found us through our online profile. Cindy was in her thirties. She was married, but separated from her husband. She already had two children from a previous relationship, one of which was almost a teenager. The father of her unborn baby was a man she had an on-again, off-again relationship with for twelve years. He was abusive and in jail for assault. Cindy was unable to work due to injuries sustained from a car accident, where her boyfriend was driving drunk. She had struggled with drug and alcohol abuse and was a member of Alcoholics Anonymous (AA) and Narcotics Anonymous (NA). She was also bipolar and had been undergoing medical treatment for her disorder. Her mother had custody of her other two children. Cindy wanted her unborn baby to have a great life and didn't want her child to go to social services with an unknown future. She asked us to meet her at a restaurant near her home, which was about an hour from where we lived.

Cindy was very nice and our personalities seemed to click right away. She sat across from us in a restaurant booth. We offered to buy her dinner, but all she ordered was lemonade. As Cindy sat sipping her lemonade, we could tell she seemed nervous. We told her right away that we were feeling nervous too. This helped break the ice and get the conversation going. Don't be afraid to admit how you are feeling when meeting with a prospective birth mom. You don't need to try to be perfect or hold in your thoughts and feelings. It is always better that she sees you as human and gets a sense of who you really are. No one is looking for someone perfect to be their child's parents. What they are looking for is someone who will cherish their baby and love him or her as their own. They are also looking for some commonalities between themselves and the adoptive parents, such as similar interests, hobbies, family backgrounds, and/or appearance.

Cindy said we resembled her own family, and she felt comfortable with us. She also wanted to know about our ancestral roots and was intrigued that I am part Italian and Paul is part German, because she is Italian and German. In addition, she told us that her grandfather was a farmer, just like Paul's grandpa.

As we continued our conversation, she asked us more questions about our backgrounds to determine if we were a good fit. She also revealed she was having a girl and wanted to know how we felt about that. We told her we always wanted a girl and were thrilled. She even asked us what baby names we were considering and approved of the choices we mentioned. Cindy also said she would want me to accompany her to doctor's appointments and be present at the birth. I happily agreed. She seemed very serious about adoption and said she was working with an adoption attorney and was eager to select a family. All went well, and we left our meeting feeling confident that we may soon be parents.

We actually did hear from our agency that Cindy had chosen us to be the parents of her child. We were very excited at first. We were going to be parents to a baby girl! However, our excitement was unfortunately short lived. Just a few days later, while we were in the process of reviewing paperwork from her attorney, I received a disturbing phone call from Cindy. She was slurring her words, seemed very confused, and didn't realize that she had called me. She was telling me how she found a really nice couple to adopt her baby. I interrupted and told her she was talking to me. She seemed surprised and said she thought she was talking to her attorney. She sounded so out of sorts. I was concerned she was abusing drugs again or that her bipolar disorder was far worse than we had realized. So, as difficult and heartbreaking as it was, we decided not to proceed with the adoption.

It was certainly a tough choice to make because you never want to give up on the chance to become a parent. The opportunity was there and it felt awful to turn it down. But could we parent a child who had issues due to drugs or had inherited her mother's mental illness? We wanted to be parents so badly, but those circumstances just did not feel right to us. So we trusted our instincts and hoped that one day, we would find our child.

Then there was Emma*. She also found our profile online. Emma was in her late twenties. She was divorced and had a four-year-old daughter. She was pregnant with a boy and was looking for a family to adopt both children. She was also unable to work due to a disability and wanted her children to have a good life. Emma and I e-mailed back and forth several times. She asked me tons of questions about our religious beliefs, our parenting philosophy, our families, etc. She seemed to be pleased with the answers I had given her. She was also very forthcoming about her own family— stating that her sister was in jail for writing bad checks and that her father's family believed in incest. She said she didn't have a lot of family support to help her with her kids. She did have a boyfriend but didn't want to burden him.

Emma and I seemed to hit it off, and after several e-mails, she agreed to contact our adoption agency. She also set up a meeting with one of the social workers. Unfortunately, Emma never showed up for her meeting, and I never heard from her again. My guess is that she changed her mind or her boyfriend offered to help. Many potential birth moms are scared and unsure of their decision. You will find they all want what is best for their children and do a lot of thinking before coming to any conclusions or decisions. After Emma failed to show up at her meeting, I sent her a nice e-mail letting her know that I enjoyed talking with her and wished her well. I left the door open for further communication, if she ever wanted to contact me again, but also told her I understood and respected whatever decision she made. Then I continued on with our adoption journey, waiting and hoping for the right situation.

We were also in contact with a few other women via Parent Profiles. Beth* was in her twenties and looking for a family for her four-year-old son. She was very emotional on the phone, and I did my best to lend a sympathetic ear and help comfort and reassure her. She had already placed a baby girl for adoption before, so she was familiar with the process. She loved her son deeply, but due to dire financial circumstances, was unable to provide for him. She was obviously torn about the whole thing but wanted what was best for her son. She had asked her family for support, but they had refused, so she felt like she was out of options. Beth did meet with our agency and was moving forward with an adoption plan with another family. (We were her first choice, but my husband and I declined because we were still working with Cindy at the time.) Before Beth's adoption was completed, her family decided to help her out and she opted to continue parenting.

We also received calls from a local twenty-year-old woman, a college student from Nebraska who wanted to finish school and start her career, and a grandmother from New Orleans, who was trying to convince her daughter and son-in-law to place their unborn son for adoption because they already had a baby boy. In addition, we heard from a nineteen-year-old girl from Texas, who had just one week until her due date and seemed desperate to find a family for her baby.

As you can see, potential birth parents are all different and not necessarily young high school students. Each has a story that makes taking care of a child difficult. And they all want their children to have the best possible lives. Sometimes that choice means placing their child for adoption; other times it means parenting. There is so much thought and consideration that goes into that decision. As a potential adoptive parent, you need to be prepared to meet women who initially think adoption is the best plan but then decide otherwise.

We had several adoption leads that didn't pan out in the end. As disappointing as it was that things didn't work out, we came to understand the complex emotions that are involved when a pregnant woman tries to decide whether or not to place her baby for adoption. Keep in mind how torn a prospective birth mother will be about possibly handing her child over to complete strangers. Imagine what a difficult, overwhelming, heartbreaking experience it would be to give birth to a baby and then say good-bye and trust that someone else will love your child and raise him or her well. Adoption is definitely a highly emotional situation for everyone involved, and you can never be sure of the outcome.

Just be patient and know that one day, one of

these women may be the person you've been waiting for. You just never know when or how it will happen. The road to get there is often paved with obstacles and some unexpected turns, but that's all part of the journey. As we found, sometimes things are not always as they seem.

"What life means to us is determined not so much by what life brings to us, as by the attitude we bring to life; not so much by what happens to us, as by our reaction to what happens."
—*Lewis L. Dunnington*

CHAPTER 14: WE WERE DECEIVED

I once read an article on adoption scams that said it is very difficult to tell the difference between a potential birth mom who is legit and one who is a scammer. I learned just how true that is when we were working with "Jennifer Razo" from Corpus Christi, Texas.

She had actually contacted us and our adoption agency several times and initially seemed legitimate. She seemed very serious about adoption and was sure of her decision. She had a sweet-sounding young voice and said she was nineteen. She wanted us at the hospital for the birth, and her scheduled C-section was just a week away! Since we had little time to prepare, we quickly purchased some clothing and baby supplies and were checking prices on flights from Detroit to Corpus Christi. We were prepared to fly to Texas on a moment's notice, if necessary. We assured the scared, young girl that we would be there, and we would help in any way we could.

Then one morning "Jennifer" called me at six a.m. hysterical and crying. She said she was at the hospital and had an emergency. She needed insulin injections and had no insurance to pay for her medications. She didn't know what she was going to do. I told her we would help, but that she had to go through our agency. She also called our social worker and told her the story.

But when our agency tried to help set everything up and gave her some phone numbers for attorneys in her home state, she seemed hesitant to contact them. Then she said she had found an attorney on her own and had him call our agency. Unfortunately, he seemed unknowledgeable about how interstate adoptions worked. When our adoption agency's director asked him questions, he was unable to answer many of them. She thought something seemed fishy. She wondered if "Jennifer" was working with multiple families and hadn't actually decided on us. I decided to do some checking of my own and was shocked by what I learned.

It turns out that the sweet birth mom was going

by at least three different names and trying to get money from adoptive parents across the country. I discovered this by posting a message on one of the adoption forums to see if anyone else had been contacted by an expectant mom from Texas. I didn't use any names, but mentioned the town she was from and said our agency had reason to believe she was working with multiple families. I received several responses, all with strikingly similar stories and identical due dates, but different names. A couple of potential adoptive parents sent me private messages and even included the woman's cell phone number. And guess what? It was the same number that "Jennifer" had given us!

So the scared young girl who called our social worker and us at six a.m. because she had just spent the night in the emergency room and didn't know how she was going to pay for her medications was actually an experienced con artist. She knew how to make us feel sorry for her, and she tried everything she could think of to get us to send money. Luckily, we're smarter than that. We knew better than to send money directly to a potential birth mom—especially one who wasn't even seen by an adoption professional. Unfortunately, others I talked to did actually send money to this girl. And when they became suspicious of her motives and stopped, she stopped contacting them.

The part that bothers me most about all of this is that she played with people's emotions. She preyed on kind, loving couples who longed for a child. She exploited people who were the most vulnerable: those who had struggled with infertility and/or pregnancy loss. People who had already grieved and suffered and lost, but were opening their hearts to her and really cared.

In the end, we all lost again—hope, time, faith, the child we all thought we were flying to Texas to bring home, and for some, money. Every couple that was contacted by this woman expended a great deal of energy and emotion on this situation. And much like our past struggles to have a child, we all once again ended up with nothing.

The good news is that this con artist was eventually caught and went to jail for her crimes. And we learned a valuable lesson about trust and the power of communication during the adoption process. By staying in close contact with our adoption agency and others who were trying to adopt, we were able to find out the truth about this woman before we spent our money on a plane ticket and ended up heartbroken.

The lesson in all of this: it is important during the adoption process to remain as rational as possible. You're going to feel a lot of emotions. When a potential birth parent contacts you crying because she is hurt, confused, and conflicted, you're going to want to reach out and comfort her. You're going to want to help. It's human nature to want to help someone in need. But what you need to remember is to be careful. Most of the women who call you will be genuine. Just make sure you don't fall for the tricks of the ones that aren't.

Typically, a pregnant woman who is seriously

considering adoption will be willing to take your adoption agency's phone number. She will be interested in learning more about the process. She will usually have questions for you. Her priority will not be the money she needs; it will be the precious child she is carrying. If a woman contacts you and seems desperate for money, that raises a red flag. Please remember that money should never be exchanged between the adoptive parents and birth parents directly. For your protection, all funds should be arranged and distributed through a licensed adoption agency or attorney.

If you follow these guidelines and remain cautious but receptive, you'll be more likely to have a successful experience.

*"Once you make a decision,
the universe conspires to make it happen."*
—*Ralph Waldo Emerson*

CHAPTER 15: THE CALL

At some point during the adoption process, most likely after a few false starts, you will get the call you've been waiting for. For us, it came on Friday, November 11, 2005. It started out as an ordinary day. And then the phone rang.

It was our social worker. She had a potential birth mom to tell us about. The interesting part is that it was not someone who had seen our online profile, newspaper ad, or business cards. It turns out a woman we had met at our adoption agency's bowling fund-raiser heard about this girl from someone at church. She remembered us from the fund-raiser and thought we would make great parents. So this potential birth mom was being referred to us by someone we had a chance meeting with at a bowling alley one night. As our social worker described the situation to us, everything sounded good. The girl and her boyfriend were both nineteen. He was working full-time at a factory, and she was going to school. They both lived at home with their parents and didn't feel ready or able to care for a child. What made this situation even more amazing was the discovery that the potential birth mom would be delivering her baby at the same hospital I was supposed to give birth at. And the baby was a girl!

I tried not to get too excited because the expectant parents hadn't actually picked us yet, and even if they did, they could still change their minds at any time. I reminded myself of how many potential birth moms had already contacted us, but in the end backed out. Still, I had a really good feeling about this situation. I kept thinking that this was it. I told our social worker that we were definitely interested. She said she was meeting with the couple soon and would show them our profile.

I hung up the phone feeling hopeful but still guarding my heart. I called my husband at work, but he didn't answer. As I left a message on his voice mail, I realized I was starting to sound excited. After I called him, I prayed. Next, I called my sister. She didn't answer either. I then called my mom, but she was still at work. I sent e-mails to some of our family and friends. By the time I finished doing all of this, I was shaking and practically in tears. My attempts to guard my heart and not get too excited had failed.

But how could I not be excited? After all the struggles we faced trying to become parents, this tiny bit of hope was like a bright star in a dark sky. I couldn't just ignore it and pretend it wasn't there.

So even though I had no way of knowing if this would work out, I still allowed myself to bask in the moment. I enjoyed the little bit of hope. I clung to it and prayed that it would bring us to the child we waited so long for.

After our social worker met with the couple, they did seem interested in us, but were still uncertain of their decision. During the meeting, the girl was very weepy and emotional, and our social worker had some doubts of whether or not she would follow through with an adoption plan. The girl's boyfriend wanted to marry her and raise the baby, but agreed to go along with whatever she decided.

Although the situation sounded uncertain, I still had a strong feeling that everything would work out for us. I can't explain why. I just believed all along that this was it.

Sometime in early December, our social worker called to tell us the couple had decided to proceed with an adoption plan and wanted us to parent their baby. We were thrilled! The approaching holiday made it even more special. We dreamed about spending the next Christmas with our precious child. We remarked at what a wonderful Christmas gift it was to learn that we might actually be parents soon!

After hearing the good news, we entered the next stage of the adoption process: more waiting.

As you'll find, if you decide to adopt, adoption is always about waiting and wondering. Once our wait to be matched with a potential birth mom was finally over, the real—and most difficult—wait began. We were now waiting for the baby to be born and wondering if the expectant couple would follow through with their adoption plans.

While we were waiting, I did some reading about adoption to pass the time. I came across a statistic that 50 percent of birth parents who make an adoption plan change their minds. I don't know what research that figure is based on or how accurate it is, but it scared me anyway. Having the birth parents change their minds was one of my biggest fears. It was even more alarming to think that our chances of bringing home a baby were the equivalent of a coin toss! And even if we did bring the baby home, we would still need to wait until the birth parents went to court (possibly a month later) before we would know that the child was staying with us. We knew things could go either way, but were hoping the odds were more in our favor than not.

They seemed to be. The potential birth parents had already considered parenting and felt that they weren't ready. They'd thought about adoption and discussed it a great lengths. The expectant mom's parents were very supportive. But there is just never any way to know how things will turn out in the end. Once a birth mom has the baby and holds her, it can change everything. We just had to wait and see and hope for the best.

For me, this wait was far harder than the wait

to be matched because there was nothing I could really do in the meantime. I no longer needed to network to find a potential birth mom. I didn't need to search for children on the Internet. I couldn't have a baby shower or even run out and buy cute baby girl clothes. I couldn't e-mail or call the potential birth mom to see how she was doing or how she was feeling, since she opted for no direct contact. I couldn't even let myself feel the excitement soon-to-be parents feel, for fear I would be heartbroken if things didn't work out. So I was forced to wait—for more than a month. Although the due date was just around the corner, it seemed like an eternity.

For the next six weeks of my life, I was eagerly waiting. First, I waited to hear how the expectant mom's pregnancy was progressing. I waited for the call that she was in labor. I waited for the precious baby girl to be born. Most importantly, I waited to see if I would become this baby's mom.

*"Compassion is the awareness of a deep bond
between yourself and all creatures."*
—*Eckhart Tolle*

CHAPTER 16: STRENGTH FROM UNEXPECTED SOURCES

There's no doubt the wait to adopt is a difficult one, but the support and encouragement you receive during the process is phenomenal. I was so touched by the many prayers, well wishes, advice, and adoption leads we received from numerous friends and family members. It was as if we had a huge cheering section, inspiring us to press forward and helping us to believe we could do this. Even in our moments of doubt and discouragement, so many people told us they had faith we would become parents. They were certain that it would happen for us one day.

Even complete strangers who I had met online at the adoption forums said the kindest words and helped me believe in myself. I had never considered myself a strong person, even though friends and family had told me I am. I'd always wondered how they could possibly think I'm strong when I'm so emotional. I seem to feel things and be affected by people and events more than the typical person. Thanks to some touching words from women who had been following our adoption story, I learned that being emotional is not synonymous with being weak. I read numerous comments from others about the strength and determination I'd shown throughout our difficult journey to become parents. A few people even told me that I inspire them! Here are some comments that I found especially helpful and encouraging. Hopefully, they will help inspire and encourage you as well.

"Envision what you want. Don't hold back. Picture as much as you can and hold on to that every day, when you lay down to rest and when you wake up in the morning. The wonderful feeling you will get thinking about how your baby will smell, feel, and sound will carry you through the wait time. It does for me. I picture how soft his or her skin will be, and I can almost hear the gurgling noises babies make. It's euphoric!"
—D, waiting to adopt

"Hang in there, Deanna. You will find a way. We pray for you and Paul every day. You are stronger than the evil in the world."

—Anonymous, after hearing about the woman from Texas who tried to scam us

"Dee, even though I am fairly new to the boards, I felt a surge of excitement reading about your two possibilities back-to-back. I'm so sad for you that they are coming out this way, but your strength is very admirable and encouraging."

—H, adoption forum member

"I'm inspired by your continued dedication to finding your child, and your determination to stay positive. I know both are extremely hard to maintain (even though you've shown such grace)...so my hat's off to you and your resolute spirit."

—C, soon-to-be adoptive parent

After reading these comments, I quickly remembered that despite the sadness and disappointments, I still kept pressing forward and refused to give up. I was driven to find my child! And that is a true indication of inner strength and determination.

You'll find too, if you choose to adopt, that you are stronger than you had ever imagined. You will be able to deal with the uncertainty, the disappointments, and the ups and downs of the adoption process. And why wouldn't you? Surviving a miscarriage can make you stronger and ready to fight for what you want in life. It brings out that survivor instinct in you. It makes you want to take charge of your life and do whatever is necessary to have the child you so desire. It also guides you to reach out to others and include them in your journey. Remember the saying that there is strength in numbers? You'll learn just how true that is when you are trying to adopt.

You'll find comfort knowing that you are never alone in the adoption process. Others are always willing to help in any way they can—whether it's connecting you with a potential lead, praying for you, spreading the word about your desire to adopt, or lending an ear when you need someone to talk to. And sometimes someone will say just the right words you need to hear to help you understand why the wait to become a parent is so long and difficult.

I had an experience that really helped make sense of our struggles to have a child. Not long after we were matched with birth parents, I was at my aunt Sharon's house for my cousin Melissa's shower. One of my other aunts, Nancy, was there and said to me, "God has a very special baby in mind for you and that's why you've had to wait so long."

My aunt had been battling neck cancer for the past year. She had been through radiation, several rounds of chemo, hospitalizations, and a lot of sickness. But through it all, her spirit had remained unbreakable, and she had never lost her sense of humor. Just a few days before this family gathering, we heard the sad news that Aunt Nancy was losing her battle with cancer and had only three months to live. As the family cried, she told everyone not to worry, that she would be fine. She planned to live life to the fullest in her final days. She believed that everyone was put on this earth for a purpose and that she had fulfilled hers.

Before getting sick, my aunt devoted her life to taking care of others. She had a big, kind heart and was always there for those who needed her. Even while she was very ill, she still thought of others and always had an encouraging word for everyone. Her courage, strength, determination, and spirit inspired me and all those around her.

That day, Aunt Nancy told me she believed that this baby was "the one." She had followed our adoption story with great interest and hope, and had always told me she knew everything would work out. We all joined hands and prayed right there in the living room. We prayed for the baby, her birth parents, and for us. We prayed that everything would work out the way it was supposed to. I got tears in my eyes because I could feel the love and support in the room that day. I felt uplifted and inspired. Everything felt right to me, and I left there knowing in my heart that I would soon become a mom.

After what my aunt said, everything seemed to

make more sense. We all have a life journey and a purpose. There are certain things that are meant to be and others that are not. My miscarriages, as devastating as they were, happened for a reason. I couldn't see it at the time. It just seemed so unfair that I lost two babies. You are probably feeling the same way. You may be wondering, "Why me?" It doesn't make sense why you should have to suffer, especially when you never did anything to deserve it. But, as I discovered, those difficult experiences shape you into the person you were destined to become. In my case, the miscarriages sent me on a different path, which would ultimately turn out to be the right one.

Just remember as you work through your feelings regarding your loss and decide what is next to always trust your instincts. Do what feels right to you. If adoption feels like the path you are drawn to, then pursue it with all the passion and enthusiasm you can. If there is another choice that feels right, then do that. I've found throughout my quest to become a mom that whenever I relied on my intuition and followed my heart, I always ended up in the right place. You will too, even if it's not the place you originally wanted or expected to be. One day it will all make sense to you. For us, it came on a snowy day in winter 2006.

"Every child begins the world again."
—Henry David Thoreau

CHAPTER 17: THE DAY SHE WAS BORN

We awoke to a fresh blanket of snow, which gently covered the grass and trees. My husband grabbed his camera to capture the beautiful and peaceful scene that greeted us the day baby Katie was due to be born. We thought this first photo would be a special memory to share with Katie someday.

We continued to enjoy the scenery through our window while eating breakfast. We chatted about the day ahead and remarked at how we couldn't believe we had gotten to this point. We would actually be heading to the hospital later in the day for the birth of a precious baby girl. We were nervous and excited, happy and sad. We knew that it would be an emotional day for both the birth family and us. We had no idea how they would react or what to expect.

Paul headed off to work, leaving me alone with my thoughts and eager anticipation. I sat at my computer reading and trying to pass the time. I was very distracted and had trouble concentrating on anything but the upcoming birth and meeting with the birth parents. A million thoughts ran through my mind that morning. I hoped the birth mom was doing well and would have an easy labor and safe delivery. I hoped all would go smoothly at the hospital when we met the birth parents for the first time. Of course, I couldn't help but wonder, what if they don't like us? What if they change their minds? I prayed several times that morning for the birth family, for the baby, and for us. Every time the phone rang—which was many times—I jumped. Is this it?

The first several times, it was a family member asking, "Did you hear anything yet?" Over and over, I replied, "No, nothing yet, but I will be sure to call you when I have news." My family was just as excited and anxious as I was!

The actual call to head to the hospital came just after lunch. "It's time," our social worker said. My heart leaped with excitement. I couldn't believe the moment had finally come. We were about to head to the hospital for the birth of our child. "Is this really it?" I wondered.

Paul had planned to come home from work around lunchtime, unless he heard from me sooner.

Luckily, he was at home when the phone rang, so we were able to jump in the car right away.

At the hospital, we met the birth parents' families for the first time in the waiting room. The birth mom's parents were both there, and so were the birth dad's mom and sister. They were all very nice and friendly. They asked us a few questions and seemed to warm up to us right away. The birth dad's sister remarked how I looked as nervous as the birth mom, and we all had a good laugh. The birth mother's parents told us how they truly believed their daughter was making the right decision, but that they were emotionally torn. Although they never actually cried in front of us, their eyes filled with tears several times. Mine did also. I really felt for them and how difficult this whole experience must be. I was somewhat relieved that they seemed very glad to meet us and said their daughter would be reassured once she got to meet us also.

About an hour later, the birth dad's mom told us that the couple was ready to meet us. "This is it," I thought nervously to myself. I felt a mix of emotions—anticipation, excitement, fear, and sadness. I knew this was an important moment that would forever change the course of several lives. I wondered what our future daughter's birth parents would think of us. Would they still feel sure about their decision? Would our personalities click?

We entered the room to find a young, attractive couple who obviously cared deeply about each other. They briefly explained their reasons for adoption: they were unable to care for a baby at this point in their lives or provide her with the life they wanted her to have. There was so much sadness on their faces, and it was clear they loved the baby and wanted the very best for her. We told them how grateful we were to them for giving us this incredible opportunity. Katie's birth mom gave me a pair of purple knit baby booties that her friend had made. She also asked if she could give us a pink stuffed Care Bear that she had since she was a small child. It was faded and wore a cute little pinned diaper. We could tell the bear was very special to her. "I thought she should have it," she said. She also gave us a few pictures of herself and her boyfriend, so Katie would know what they looked like.

I gave Katie's birth mom a gift basket with bath products and nail polish, a small token of our appreciation. Although I felt there was nothing we could ever give her to express our gratitude, she seemed to like the gesture. We talked for a few minutes and then returned to the waiting room.

We spent the next couple of hours in the waiting room with the birth parents' families. You would think this would be a very awkward time for all of us, since we were practically strangers, but surprisingly it wasn't. I guess it was because we were all connected to this precious child that was about to be born. We all had her best interests at heart. We all cared about what happened and wanted the best possible outcome. Having a common interest made us feel less like strangers.

Once the baby was born, the birth mom's parents told us to come to her room with them. As much as I wanted to just jump up and go, my heart told me otherwise. As hard as it was, I thought it was important that they have some time alone first with their daughter and the baby. It just felt like the right thing to do. They needed some privacy and a little time to process the whole experience and spend time with the precious baby.

"You go first," I said. "Just come back and get us when you are ready."

They seemed surprised, but thanked us, and hurried off to meet the new baby.

About twenty minutes later (possibly the longest twenty minutes of my life), the birth mom's parents returned. The first thing they said to us was "Are you ready to meet *your* baby?" We nodded and headed with them to the room.

Finally, the moment we had been waiting for had arrived! Seven years of hoping, praying, searching, and wondering had led up to this day. I really had no idea what to expect or how I would feel. I had always imagined crying great tears of joy when I held my baby in my arms for the first time. But adoption is a different experience than giving birth. It isn't just about you and your family. It is the coming together of two separate families. There are additional emotions and concerns involved. It isn't just a day of celebration; it is a day of facing reality and letting go.

Meeting baby Katie was bittersweet. She was so beautiful and precious. We couldn't believe she was finally here. Of course, we were so thrilled to meet her. On the other hand, we were very sad for her birth parents. It just tore me up inside to know that as we were preparing for one of the most exciting and happy times in our lives, they were preparing to let go and say good-bye. While we were celebrating the birth of our first child, they would be grieving the loss of theirs. There was so much powerful and conflicting emotion in the room—both joy and sorrow.

Katie's birth mother was holding her when we entered the room, and shortly after handed her to me. As I held Katie in my arms for the first time, I felt an immediate bond and overwhelming sense of awe and love. I remembered thinking, "This baby is my daughter. She is the answer to all my prayers." Then I quickly snapped back to reality and remembered that nothing was certain yet. Her birth parents could still change their minds. A wave of fear came over me, as I realized that the future I had planned could still come crashing down around me. But that was a chance I was willing to take. Putting my heart on the line was necessary in order to have the opportunity to be a mother to this precious baby girl.

While we were all in the hospital room that afternoon, we asked if it would be okay to take a couple of pictures of the baby with her birth parents. I wanted to capture the whole experience so that we could share it with Katie one day. Katie's birth parents agreed to pose for a couple of pictures. Then their families also got pictures of us with baby Katie. Shortly after, we all hugged like old friends. For some reason, it felt natural to do this, even though we had just met hours before. We were two families connected by our love for a child.

After our visit, the nurse took the baby to the nursery. The hospital staff was fabulous and very understanding. As an adoptive parent, I was given a hospital wristband so that I could have access to the nursery to visit and care for the baby. It was identical to the bracelet Katie's birth mom had. I was surprised and grateful for the way the hospital staff treated us. Although I was not a patient and had not just given birth, I had all the privileges and treatment of a new mom. The nurses gave me a diaper bag and samples of baby formula. They also gave us a special handmade blanket and two knitted hats. One nurse explained that the blanket was a gift from the staff to special babies. I was touched by their thoughtfulness.

My husband and I were allowed to spend as much time in the nursery with the baby as we wanted. We both held and rocked her. The nurse gave the baby her first bath, and we took pictures. I changed and fed Katie. It felt just like I had imagined having a new baby would feel. We were already bonding, and by the end of the night, we found it very difficult to leave Katie at the hospital and go home. I longed to take her home with us.

We returned as soon as we could the next morning, eager to spend time with the precious baby girl. That day, the birth parents' mothers came to the nursery to visit. Katie's birth mom's parents also gave us a baby gift, a cute little Winnie the Pooh outfit with a tiny hat. Their card said, "Enjoy your baby." I was not expecting a gift from them and thought it was a very nice gesture.

That day we also changed Katie into her "going-home" outfit, which was a lavender fleece one-piece pajama set with feet. The nurse arranged for a photographer to come in and take a professional picture, which is something they do for all new babies born at that particular hospital. Toward the end of the day, Katie was released from the hospital, and we eagerly headed home to start our lives as a new family.

I'll never forget the breathtaking feeling of pure joy and exhilaration I experienced as I walked out of the hospital that afternoon holding our tiny, precious baby in her car seat. I just couldn't stop smiling. It was clearly one of the best moments of my entire life. Everything I had been through, all that I had wished for and planned for, led up to this moment. It felt like a dream come true.

If you ask any adoptive parent what it was like to see and meet their child for the first time, they will all tell you heartwarming stories of pure joy and overwhelming love. It is a precious memory that is beautifully etched in your mind and forever changes your life.

Jason Bradley-Krauss will never forget the breathtaking moment he saw his children for the first time.

"It was perhaps the most profound and phenomenal moment of my life," says Jason.

"Whenever I think of that day, I can visualize the scene as if it is happening all over again. I can still feel the intensity of the light on my skin. I can feel and smell the air. It's like I had reached an emotional apex, where overwhelming love, worry, hopes, and dreams collide."

My wish is that you will one day experience this kind of joy. Becoming a parent is an incredible and miraculous experience unlike any other. The good news is that there are many options for creating a family, so you don't need to feel discouraged if one way doesn't work for you. You have choices. No matter what challenges or obstacles you've faced, you *can* become a parent.

*"If one advances confidently in the direction
of his dreams, and endeavors to live the life
which he has imagined, he will meet
with success unexpected in common hours."*
—*Henry David Thoreau*

CHAPTER 18: HAPPILY EVER AFTER?

There's no doubt that bringing Katie home from the hospital was a monumental moment in our lives. We couldn't wait to settle into our new roles as parents. We had many visitors the first night Katie was home. My parents, mother-in-law, sister, brother-in-law, niece, and nephew all came over to meet and hold our precious daughter. Although we were at the hospital caring for Katie since shortly after her birth, we did not have our families come to see her there. We wanted to respect the birth parents' privacy and give them time to deal with their decision. It didn't feel right to celebrate our daughter's birth while her biological family was grieving their loss. In order for us to have this child, they had to let her go. We know that must have been heartbreaking and extremely difficult for them. So we saved our family celebration until we got home.

Since our families had been eagerly waiting for two days to meet our sweet baby, they were very excited. We took lots of pictures that night. And, of course, everyone took turns holding her—even our four-year-old niece Ashley. In fact, Ashley was the most thrilled of all. She already had a terrific little brother, so she felt like this girl cousin was like a little sister. The smile on Ashley's face was priceless. Turns out, there were lots of smiles that night. None of us could help being filled with joy!

After visiting with our families, we were all exhausted and settled in for the night. Like most new parents, it was a night filled with frequent feedings, lots of crying, and very little sleep. But I was definitely up for the challenge! I had anticipated and prepared for this for a very long time. I was eager to learn and discover our new daughter's personality and temperament. I was ready to do whatever I could to ensure she was happy, healthy, and showered with love.

It turned out she was a feisty, intelligent, and observant baby. She liked to look around at her environment and enjoyed being held and rocked. To calm her down, I would play a children's music CD and dance around with her in my arms. She really seemed to love this. I would also sing to her. I even made up my own little tunes for her: "Katie Girl" and "Katie, Katie, the Pretty Little Lady."

I quickly found in the days that followed that our daughter didn't like to sleep unless someone was holding her. She slept only in increments of fifteen minutes at a time, day and night. If I held her, she would sleep an hour or more. I was so sleep deprived that after three days of having her home, I had only slept a total of four hours. And I'm not talking four hours per night! The first night, I got a mere fifteen minutes of sleep. But the amazing part is that I didn't care and was miraculously still functioning. I was elated. My adrenaline was high. I was pouring my heart and soul into being the best mom I could possibly be. Katie gave my life meaning and purpose. I enjoyed holding her close; gently kissing her tiny, soft cheek; rocking her and singing lullabies; feeding her; and looking at her beautiful, precious face. Every time she cried, I would spring to my feet and run to her side. I couldn't wait to comfort her. I loved being a new mom! It was the most marvelous feeling to love and care for a baby. It was everything I had imagined and more.

My husband Paul was also adjusting well to being a new dad. He was no longer afraid of being a parent and seemed genuinely interested in his new role. His was very responsive to Katie's cries as well. Several times we both jumped from the bed when we heard her during the night. Paul also spent time bonding with Katie by watching The Weather Channel together while I got some much-needed rest. He would explain things to her just like she was a little adult, instead of a baby. It was so heartwarming to watch. She actually seemed very attentive and appeared to be listening. Paul would even feed Katie her bottle occasionally and liked to hold and rock her too. Sometimes we would teasingly fight over who got to hold her.

Katie's lively, charming personality delighted us daily, and we were often surprised by her ability to learn quickly. Her love for music was also apparent at a very early age. At just a few weeks old, we were amazed to see her tiny, little hand tapping perfectly to the beat of a song. We both just looked at each other in disbelief. How was it possible for a baby so young to do that? Little did we know, she would one day become a talented dancer and learn to play piano at age six.

We were really enjoying our new daughter and the many ways parenthood was enriching our lives. We bonded with her immediately, and it felt as if we had been together forever. No one would have guessed that we were not biologically related. Our love for our daughter was just as strong and deep as it would have been had she been born to us.

But did this mean we would live happily ever after? Well, not just yet. Although we were happy and relieved we had gotten this far in the adoption process, we knew our journey wasn't quite over yet. For those of you who are unfamiliar with domestic adoption, it doesn't end once you have the baby in your home. There are still a few details that remain before the adoption will be finalized and you are legally named your child's parents.

You are probably wondering, "How can you bring a child home from the hospital when she isn't actually yours yet?" The answer is: the birth parents will sign a paper at the hospital that appoints you and your spouse the child's legal guardians. You will be responsible for the baby's care, and the birth parents will retain their rights as parents. During your time as a legal guardian, the biological parents can choose to back out of the adoption and ask that the baby be returned to them. They have the option to do this until they go to court and relinquish their rights as parents. The process is called "a termination of parental rights" and will legally free the child to be adopted. How soon relinquishment happens depends on the laws of the state the baby is born in. In Michigan, the birth parents typically go to court in about a month or two. In our case, it was about seven weeks.

Of course, during those seven weeks, we were so busy loving and caring for our baby. Our bond with her strengthened each day. It was difficult to imagine how we could ever give our child back to her birth parents if they changed their minds. I knew we would be so heartbroken and devastated if this happened. But I also knew that loving this precious amazing baby was worth the risk. Sometimes you just need to put your heart on the line to experience what life has in store for you.

When the court day finally came, it seemed like time stood still for a while. I sat on pins and needles for hours, anxiously waiting to hear from our social worker. She and Katie's birth parents were all in court for the termination of parental rights. She promised she would call as soon as the hearing was over.

My husband was at work that day, which made the time pass even more slowly. I had no adults around to have a conversation with, no one to share my thoughts and feelings. I kept thinking and praying that everything would work out. I believed in my heart that all would go well, and that as difficult as it was, Katie's biological parents would sign the relinquishment papers. Still, there was a part of me that knew it wasn't official and that everything could change.

I imagined what it must feel like to be on the other side of the adoption process. How heartbreaking it must be to give up your rights to your child after carrying her for nine months, giving birth, and then meeting and holding her! There's obviously a very strong attachment between a mother and her child, even before she is born. To give that up is a loss that a biological parent carries with her for the rest of her life. Would Katie's birth mom be strong enough and willing to withstand that kind of pain? Did she feel confident that we could provide the stable, loving home that she had envisioned for her child?

My answer came early that afternoon. Our social worker called. "They signed," she told me. What a relief it was to hear those words! I started to cry. Our adoption worker said that it was a very emotional day for Katie's birth parents and their families. There were a lot of tears in the courtroom that day. This was always the hardest part of adopting for me. To know that our joy came out of someone else's pain makes me feel sad and guilty inside. But as our adoption worker explained, "You didn't take anything from her. She *gave* you this gift because she wanted to."

That is one thing that all birth parents have in common. Their decision to place their babies for adoption is made out of love. They want the best possible life for their children and realize that, for whatever reason, they are unable to provide the kind of life they believe their kids deserve to have. As difficult as it is, they look for a family that they believe will offer their babies a good, stable, loving home and a promising future. This extraordinary gift of life is one of the most selfless acts of love that I could ever imagine.

A young woman who we had met briefly in the hospital had given us the best gift in the entire world. She gave us a child. She provided me with the experience of being a mother. She offered us the opportunity to love, nurture, teach, protect, support, and care for another human life. What an amazing leap of faith she took to entrust her child to virtual strangers! My heart just fills with gratitude and appreciation whenever I think of what our daughter's birth mom gave to us. I will be forever thankful to her and for the day that sealed our fate.

After our daughter's birth parents signed the papers relinquishing their parental rights, we entered the final phase of the adoption process called "post-placement and finalization." When you get to this point, you'll most likely find it to be the easy part. During the next six months, your social worker will visit a few times and write a report on how the baby is growing, developing, and adjusting to her new home. These papers are submitted to the court as proof that all is going well and that the adoption is in the baby's best interests. There is no need to worry that the adoption won't work out at this point. The post-placement period is mostly a formality, and the majority of adoptions do go through unless there is a serious problem.

After the post-placement visits are complete, you will need to write a letter to the court requesting that the adoption be finalized. Your social worker will also write a letter recommending you as parents. Next, a court date is scheduled to finalize the adoption. We went to court in mid-September 2006, which was about eight months after bringing our daughter home from the hospital.

At the finalization hearing, you, your spouse, your child, and your social worker will meet with a judge in a county court. Our adoption hearing took place at a local court in Michigan. I must admit I was a bit nervous and intimidated at first. I had served on jury duty twice, once in downtown Detroit at the federal court building and once in the very same county court that our adoption was scheduled to take place in. But I had never appeared before a judge for my own hearing. It was such an important day in my life. I wanted everything to go well. When we met the judge, I was relieved he turned out to be a very kind man, and he was happy to assist us. I imagine adoption finalization is probably one of the more pleasant hearings for a judge.

Family members are also welcome to attend and witness the hearing. My mom, sister, and niece came to court that day. During the hearing, you will answer questions about your ability and desire to be the baby's parents. The judge will decide if the adoption is in the baby's best interest and agree to finalize. Then the judge will sign papers that officially make you and your spouse your child's legal parents. From this moment on, your baby will be a part of your family forever. Her birth family can't reclaim her or change their minds. No one else can adopt her. She is now *your* child—not just in your heart, but also in the eyes of the law. As part of the finalization, you will also receive a new copy of your child's birth certificate in the mail. The birth certificate will list you as the baby's parents.

Once the finalization papers were signed, the judge congratulated us and shook our hands. Our adoption worker gave us a hug. We then posed for pictures with them to remember this important day in our family.

As you can imagine, the day you finalize your adoption is an exciting time worth celebrating. Some adoptive parents refer to it as "Gotcha Day." We prefer to call it "Adoption Day." Most families will do something special to honor this important day in your family's life. We went to lunch at Applebee's and then took our daughter to the park and beach. We took pictures of our happy family and held our daughter close. It was a moment we will forever treasure. Our long journey to become parents had finally ended.

When you reach the end of your journey, you will be filled with a sense of peace, love, and happiness. Your life will begin to make sense for the first time in a very long time. You may be wondering what I mean by this. All I can say is that you will have a better understanding of who you are and the important lessons life has given you. Sure, you've been through many struggles and pain that seemed unfair. Certainly, no one can argue that you've faced some very sad and unfortunate circumstances in your past. No one should have to bear the pain of losing a child. No one should have to fight to become a parent. But these life events exist. We always question why there is pain, loss, suffering, and heartbreak in the world. Although there is no simple answer, these situations exist because they are part of our life experience. We are all here to learn, grow, and experience all that life has to offer. We must take the good with the bad and try to learn from it.

What I learned from my pregnancy losses and our daughter's adoption is this: sometimes when life doesn't work out as you planned, there is a greater force at work. There may be lessons you need to learn, or your circumstances may be leading you to a different path—the one you were meant to take.

"Adoption is a blessing. It's a life full of all new possibilities, bringing hope, fulfilling dreams, and full of love," says adoptive mother Christina Molby. "As we continue our journey through what life brings us, I remain with an open heart and mind, as we explore what our life's purpose or meaning really is."

There is no doubt in my mind that my daughter was meant to be a part of our family. The way everything came together was just incredible and miraculous. I have no explanation for how it all panned out. But I do know that it just felt right. I am convinced that I was led to adoption for a reason. I was directed to that path so I could be the mother of a particular child. And if I had to do it all over again, I wouldn't change a thing.

Like I wrote in a picture book I created of my daughter's adoption story:

"Even though you weren't born to us, you grew in our hearts. We will be forever connected because love is what makes a family."

When you get your own happy ending, you will know deep inside that everything you have experienced was all in preparation for this moment—the one monumental point in time where everything finally is as it should be. You will feel complete and whole at last, like the missing piece of your heart has been found. And once your child has captured your heart, she will be there forever!

QUESTIONS AND ANSWERS

If you're considering adoption, you'll likely have many questions and concerns. This Q&A will answer frequently asked questions about adoption, as well as address some common misconceptions many people have.

Isn't domestic infant adoption rare?

Actually, domestic infant adoption is a lot more common than most people realize. According to the National Council for Adoption (NCFA), approximately 22,000 babies are adopted annually through domestic infant adoption. I know several families who have adopted successfully in the metro Detroit area alone.

The thing about domestic adoption is that you might not even realize that a child you meet was adopted, unless the family mentions it. As I said, when someone meets our family for the first time, they automatically assume that our daughter is our biological child. They even look for similarities between her and us. I've heard several times how Katie is tall like her dad or how she is compassionate like her mom. You're actually very likely to encounter a family who adopted domestically, whether you realize it or not.

If you're interested in domestic newborn adoption, know that it is definitely possible and is certainly not a rarity. From personal experience, I can also tell you that domestic newborn adoption is a terrific way to build your family. Not only will you have a precious child to love and care for, but often you will be able to begin bonding with your new baby very early in his or her life.

Some adoptive parents have the opportunity to be present at the birth or even in the room while the baby is being born. Others meet their children shortly after birth. All appreciate being able to be a part of their child's life as soon as possible. Other than giving birth yourself or hiring a surrogate, there is no other form of parenthood that allows you to bond with your baby as early in his or her life. Domestic newborn adoption is an extraordinary blessing with many similarities to creating a family in the traditional way.

Isn't adoption expensive?

Although some adoptions can be expensive, such as international adoptions where travel is required or domestic adoptions where there are a lot of birth parent expenses, most are not as costly as you might think. Adoption is certainly not reserved for the rich or privileged. In fact, the majority of people I know who adopted their children are average middle-class families.

According to *Adoptive Families* magazine, the cost of adopting domestically in the United States in 2011 was $20,000–$40,000. But that doesn't mean that you will have to cover the entire bill up-front or by yourself. Most agencies have a fee schedule that outlines how much money is due at various stages throughout the process, so you don't have to worry about needing a large sum of money at once. In addition, some employers provide adoption assistance to help with the costs. And there are a variety of adoption grants and loans available to qualifying applicants.

When we adopted in 2006, our total costs including the home study, agency fees, and our own advertising expenses totaled approximately $15,000. Keep in mind that this figure doesn't include the federal per child adoption tax credit. We received a reimbursement from the U.S. government of approximately $10,000 after adopting our daughter. In 2012, the tax credit was $12,650 per child. Unfortunately, this credit ended on December 31, 2012. It is uncertain whether or not a general adoption tax credit will be offered again in the future. However, in 2013, there was still a $6,000 federal adoption tax credit for those who adopt special needs children from foster care.

Also, remember that adopting from the foster care system is relatively inexpensive to begin with and may just cost the price of a home study. If you are on a tight budget or just want to adopt a child in need or a sibling group, foster care adoption is definitely worth checking into.

What is required for a domestic adoption?

Here is a list of what you'll likely need if you choose to do a domestic adoption:

- A completed preliminary and formal application, along with application fees

- A home study, which includes three to four visits in your home with a social worker

- Financial documents, including bank statements, credit card statements, income tax returns, pay stubs, and mortgage and loan balances

- A list of assets and liabilities, including monthly payments for your house, cars, utilities, groceries, gas, and entertainment, as well as the value of your home, cars, and other assets

- Letters from your employers with employment and salary verification, health insurance coverage info, and other benefit details

- Reference letters from friends, family, and coworkers who can attest to your character and ability to parent a child

- Complete physicals and blood tests from your family doctor, including tests for HIV, hepatitis B, tuberculosis, blood pressure, hearing, and vision

- Copies of your birth certificates, driver's licenses, social security cards, and marriage license

- Detailed autobiographies about your lives, including your childhood experiences and upbringing, your relationships with your extended family, your marriage, philosophy on discipline, and attitudes regarding adoption and how you plan to explain it to your child

- Forms for credit and criminal background checks, as well as certificates of identity.

What is required for an international adoption?

The requirements for adopting internationally vary depending on which country and program you choose. In general, you will need the same documents as a domestic adoption, plus some additional paperwork. You must apply with the United States Citizenship and Immigration Services

(USCIS), formerly known as the Immigration and Naturalization Service (INS), to get approval to bring an adopted child into the United States. You'll need to complete form I-171H and also request two sets of fingerprint cards for each person.

The majority of international adoptions require a dossier, which is a collection of documents that are translated, notarized, and contain seals from your county, state, and the US government. Some of these documents are the same as the ones required by the USCIS and your home study.

For a complete list of requirements, check with the adoption agencies you're considering.

What if a birth parent wants his or her child back?

Some people mistakenly believe that a birth parent can reclaim a child years after an adoption, disrupting the child's life and leaving the adoptive parents devastated and heartbroken.

Although there have been a few very rare cases of this on television, birth parents typically cannot reclaim a child after the adoption is final. In fact, once biological parents go to court and terminate their parental rights, they have no legal claim to that child. They cannot change their minds or have a minor child come live with them. Adoption laws are designed with the child's best interests in mind. No one wants to see a happy, well-adjusted child torn from the only family he or she has ever really known. This would create such emotional turmoil and upheaval in a child's life, so the law just doesn't permit it.

Also, keep in mind that birth parents love their children and want the best possible life for them. That's part of the reason why they chose adoption in the first place. They certainly wouldn't want to hurt their kids by disrupting their lives or creating unnecessary stress.

So if you are reluctant to adopt because you fear the baby's birth parents will be some sort of a threat, you can relax. Not only are birth parents not a threat at all, they are on the *same side as you*. Both adoptive parents and biological parents want the child to be safe, happy, healthy, secure—and most of all, loved. In the majority of cases, all parties work together to create the best possible life and environment for the child. They may even have an ongoing relationship that offers everyone involved a terrific opportunity to bond and share their lives with each other.

Aren't open adoptions risky and confusing?

Some people considering adoption are afraid of open adoptions, where the birth parents and adoptive parents have ongoing contact. They may believe that children who have contact with their birth parents may become confused about who their family is or become too attached to their biological parents and want to live with them. This couldn't be further from the truth.

Children typically have a good understanding of adoption and know that biological parents gave birth to them, but adoptive parents are the ones who take care of them. Usually they call their birth parents by their first names, and call their adoptive parents "Mommy" and "Daddy." They know very well who their parents are and have no desire to switch families.

Christina Molby and her husband have an open adoption with their son's birth parents. But they didn't start out wanting or expecting that. Like many couples, they were initially afraid of open adoption. After learning more and talking to others, they became more willing to have some contact.

"At first you're more vulnerable, but as time goes by, your fears are alleviated," Christina explains. "I know I'm his mom, and nothing can change that."

When Christina and her husband were first matched with their son's birth parents, they agreed to meet with them and spend some time together. Christina had the opportunity to accompany her son's birth mom to doctor's visits and ultrasounds. She and her husband got to know both birth parents during the five months prior to their son's birth and developed a relationship with them during this time.

"When we walked away from the hospital with our son, we agreed to four visits per year," she says. "Now we couldn't imagine visiting any less than that. We love them!"

In our case, we have a semi-open adoption, which means there is some degree of openness but no ongoing visits. We met our daughter's biological family prior to her birth, and we exchange pictures and letters through our agency. In our experience, it has been a great opportunity to have some communication. Our daughter has pictures and precious letters that will assure her one day that her birth mother loves her very much. Her birth mom gets to see that her child is doing well, which helps with the grieving process and gives her reassurance that she made the right decision.

In the past when adoptions were closed, birth parents were left wondering for years if their child was okay. Times have definitely changed. Today most adoptions have some degree of openness, which can include letters and pictures, e-mails, phone calls, and even visits.

Although it may sound risky to you at first, kids who are part of an open adoption relationship will feel more secure and have fewer questions about their birth families and reasons why they were placed for adoption. They will also benefit by having more people in their life who love and cherish them. After all, you can never have too many people to love your kids!

Don't Most Adopted Children Have Special Needs?

There are certainly some adopted children with special needs. Problems can include: fetal alcohol syndrome (FAS), drug exposure, learning disabilities, attachment disorders, attention deficit hyperactivity disorder (ADHD), attention deficit disorder (ADD), oppositional defiant disorder (ODD), and mental illnesses. However, the majority of babies who are adopted are healthy and have few, if any, special needs. Most grow up to be happy, healthy, well-adjusted adults.

You are more likely to encounter a child with special needs if you adopt an older child from the foster care system because these kids often come from homes with physical or sexual abuse and/or parents with drug and alcohol addictions. Also, some children adopted internationally have development or learning delays due to living in an orphanage. But that still doesn't mean you can't have a sweet, lovable, healthy child. If you do adopt a child with special needs, providing additional support and resources can go a long way toward helping them live rewarding and fulfilling lives. Many of the challenges these kids face can be addressed with good family communication, therapy, medication, and individualized education plans (IEPs) that are available through the community and in public schools.

Will I Love My Child the Same as a Biological Child?

Will the love you have for your child be inferior to the love you would have for a biological child? Definitely not. I know a few couples who have both biological and adopted children, and they can honestly say there is no difference in the love they feel for their kids.

Christina Molby is one of these parents. Christina gave birth to her daughter and adopted her son. She admits, like most potential adoptive parents, that she initially wondered if she would feel differently about her son. Her concerns quickly vanished when he was born.

"Once you hold that baby in your arms, it's love at first sight," she explains. "The love you feel for a biological child and an adoptive child is the same."

Darlene Zeutzius, a mother of five from Wisconsin, has also experienced a very strong and loving bond with her children. Darlene and her husband suffered two miscarriages before their biological daughter was born. Several years later, they adopted four children from foster care.

"Since the very beginning, we have had an amazing bond," says Darlene. "From the very first meeting, they called us mom and dad. I think they wanted us just as much as we wanted them."

As you can see, many of the concerns people have about adopting are unfounded or based on misinformation. Hopefully, this helps to ease your fears and gives you a good idea of what adoption is really like. It is truly a positive and life-changing experience—one that I wholeheartedly recommend to anyone considering it.

RESOURCES

Here is a list of resources you may find helpful. These were all current at the time of publication. Please keep in mind that due to the changing nature of the Internet, some links may not continue to be available.

Adoption:

Adoption Associates Inc.
A Michigan-based Christian adoption agency, founded in 1990. Offers both domestic and international adoptions. Also features an in-house legal staff and travel agency.
1-800-677-2367
www.adoptionassociates.net

Adoption.com
A comprehensive site with numerous topics related to adoption. Provides articles and information for both adoptive parents and birth parents before, during, and after the adoption. Also offers support for adoptees. Features a discussion forum located at forums.adoption.com for sharing information and experiences.
www.adoption.com

The Adoption Exchange

A nonprofit child welfare organization founded in 1983 to work for safety and permanence in the lives of foster children. Offers information and resources on the adoption process, as well as post-placement services. Includes a photo listing of children from Colorado, Missouri, Nevada, New Mexico, Oklahoma, South Dakota, and Wyoming.

www.adoptex.org

Adoption Situations

A site for people who are interested in posting or reading about available adoption situations throughout the country.

www.adoptionsituations.com

Adoptive Families

Adoptive Families magazine has a wealth of information—both in their printed publication and online—for those at all stages of the adoption process. Read articles written by adoption experts and adoptive parents.

1-800-372-3300

www.adoptivefamilies.com

AdoptUSKids

A national photo listing service for children awaiting adoption across the United States. Includes many sibling groups and special needs kids in foster care.

www.adoptuskids.org

Americans for International Aid and Adoption (AIAA)

A nonprofit international adoption agency founded in 1975. The agency is licensed in the state of Michigan and specializes in adoptions from Korea, Russia, Bulgaria, and Hungary.

1-248-362-1207

www.aiaaadopt.org/

American Adoptions

A licensed nonprofit agency that works with prospective adoptive families and birth parents across the country. Offers articles for birth parents to help aid them in the decision-making process and features a photo listing of waiting adoptive parents.

1-800-ADOPTION

www.americanadoptions.com/

Bethany Christian Services

Founded in 1944, Bethany is the largest adoption agency in the United States. They have more than one hundred offices in more than thirty states. Their services include family support and preservation, adoption, foster care, pregnancy counseling, training, refugee services, sponsorship, and infertility ministry.

1-800-BETHANY

www.bethany.org

Dave Thomas Foundation for Adoption

Provides a wealth of information on foster care adoption, including free resources and publications, fund-raising events, and opportunities to raise awareness in your community. Also offers grants to adoption agencies for their assistance in placing children from foster care into loving homes.

1-800-ASK-DTFA

www.davethomasfoundation.org

Family Adoption Consultants (FAC)

FAC is licensed in Michigan and Ohio and has more than thirty years of experience. They provide adoption assistance, counseling, and support for pregnant women considering adoption and couples looking to adopt. The agency offers programs for both domestic and international adoption.

(586) 726-2988 (in Michigan)

(330) 296-2757 (in Ohio)

www.facadopt.org

Forever Families

Specializing in domestic adoption since 1997, Forever Families offers both a domestic infant program and national state ward program. The agency is licensed in Michigan and also provides assistance to families who are interested in adopting internationally.

1-866-842-5919

www.forever-families.org/

Holt International Children's Services

A Christian-based organization formed more than fifty years ago to find loving homes for orphaned and abandoned children. Also features child sponsorships and the opportunity to contribute to adoption funds and purchase memorial gifts.

1-888-355-HOLT

www.holtinternational.org/

Independent Adoption Center

A nationwide domestic open adoption center founded in 1982, with offices in California, North Carolina, Georgia, Indiana, Texas, and New York. Includes articles, blogs, answers to frequently asked questions, and more. Publishes *Open Adoption Magazine*. Also offers a sliding-scale fee schedule based on income.

1-800-877-OPEN

www.adoptionhelp.org

Lifetime Adoption Center LLC

Founded in 1986 in the state of California, Lifetime Adoption Center is a nationwide leader in domestic open adoption. Features articles, a newsletter, free informational webinars, and blogs. Also operates a twenty-four-hour hotline for birth parents and emergencies.

1-800-923-6784

www.lifetimeadoption.com

Michigan Adoption Resource Exchange (MARE)
Provides information on adopting Michigan children waiting in the foster care system. Also offers a photo listing and description of the kids, as well as a list of licensed Michigan adoption agencies.
1-800-589-6273 (in Michigan)
www.mare.org

Morning Star Adoption Center
Founded in 1987 by a group of adoptive parents, Morning Star Adoption Center is licensed in Michigan and provides home studies and consulting services to prospective adoptive parents. The agency can assist with direct placement, interstate, and international adoptions.
1-866-236-7866
www.morningstaradoption.org

National Council for Adoption (NCFA)
A nonprofit adoption advocacy organization that promotes a culture of adoption through education, research, and legislative action. NCFA serves children, birth parents, adoptive families, adult adoptees, adoption agencies, US and foreign governments, policymakers, media, and the general public.
(703) 299-6633
www.adoptioncouncil.org/

Adoption Grants and Financial Aid:

Affording Adoption Foundation
Since January 2010, the Affording Adoption Foundation (AAF) has awarded more than $27,000 in grants to families in the process of adopting.
www.affordingadoption.com

Gift of Adoption Fund
A national 501(c)3 charitable organization that provides adoption grants to qualifying hopeful parents who are approved to adopt but lack the required funds.
www.giftofadoption.org/

National Adoption Foundation
Established in 1994, the National Adoption Foundation (NAF) has helped more than 6,000 adoptive parents by providing grants, loans, and other financial assistance programs.
http://fundyouradoption.org

Depression and Anxiety:

The Anxiety and Depression Association of America

Founded in 1980, this organization's mission is to help prevent, treat, and cure anxiety and depression. Features facts on anxiety and depression, a list of commonly asked questions and misconceptions, as well as resources for getting help and helping others.

www.adaa.org

The National Alliance on Mental Illness

Research, publications, discussion groups, and support for those affected by mental disorders, including depression, anxiety, post-traumatic stress disorder, and many more. Also provides info on possible treatment plans and medications.

www.nami.org

The National Institute of Mental Health

The largest research organization in the world dedicated to mental illnesses. This comprehensive site contains news articles and educational research for various disorders, including anxiety and depression.

www.nimh.nih.gov

Miscarriage and Loss:

The American Pregnancy Association
A national health organization committed to promoting reproductive and pregnancy wellness through education, research, advocacy, and community awareness. Features information on the stages of pregnancy, as well as resources on infertility, pregnancy loss, medications, prenatal testing, women's health, and adoption.
www.americanpregnancy.org

HopeXchange
Information and support for anyone grieving the loss of a baby through miscarriage, stillbirth, or early infant death. Features articles, booklets, pamphlets, miscarriage FAQs, and a free monthly newsletter. Also offers tips, positive quotes, healing products, and music to encourage the mind and uplift the spirit.
www.hopexchange.com

Infertility and Adoption Counseling Center
Counseling, education, workshops, and emotional support to those affected by infertility and miscarriage. Helps to discuss family alternatives, including fertility treatments, donor options, adoption, surrogacy, or the child-free family.
(609) 737-8750
www.iaccenter.com

Miscarriage Matters
A nonprofit organization that offers free support and mentoring for those who have lost a child through miscarriage, stillbirth, and early infant loss.
http://www.mymiscarriagematters.com/

Miscarriage Support
Forums, blogs, videos, interviews, workbooks, and support to help couples who have miscarried. Developed by a husband after his wife miscarried several years ago.
http://miscarriagesupport.com/

Mommies Enduring Neonatal Death (MEND)
A Christian nonprofit organization that helps families who have suffered the loss of a baby through miscarriage, stillbirth, or early infant death. Features free newsletters, family memorial web pages, keepsake items, music, commemorative ceremonies, and support groups.
www.mend.org

REFERENCES

Anxiety Disorders: National Institute of Mental Health. U.S. Department of Health and Human Services, NIH Publication No. 09 3879, 2009.

Depression. U.S. Department of Health and Human Services, NIH Publication No. 11-3561, 2011.

Foley, Denise and Eileen Nechas. *Women's Encyclopedia of Health & Emotional Healing,* (Pennsylvania: Rodale Press, Inc., 1993), 278–283.

Rai, RS. Antiphospholipid syndrome and recurrent miscarriage. J Postgrad Med 2002; 48: 3–4.

ABOUT THE AUTHOR

Deanna Kahler is an award-winning author and proud mom. Her work has been published in  numerous corporate newsletters and magazines across the country. She began writing as a young child and enjoys the opportunity to reach others and make a difference in their lives.

Deanna holds a bachelor's degree in communication arts from Oakland University in Rochester, Michigan, where she graduated with departmental honors.

She lives with her husband and daughter in a metro Detroit suburb and enjoys writing, dancing, walking, and visiting parks in her spare time.

For more information about the author, please visit www.deannakahler.com.